1978

CHILDREN IN FOSTER CARE

Destitute, Neglected . . .
Betrayed

Alan R. Gruber, D.S.W.
Director of Research
Boston Children's Service
Association, Boston

HUMAN SCIENCES PRESS
72 Fifth Avenue   /   3 Henrietta Street
NEW YORK, New York 10011 / LONDON, WC2E 8LU England

Library of Congress Catalog Number 77-521

ISBN: 0-87705-281-6

Copyright © 1978 by Human Sciences Press
72 Fifth Avenue, New York, New York 10011

Printed in the United States of America
789   987654321

Library of Congress Cataloging in Publication Data

Gruber, Alan R
    Children in foster care.

    Bibliography: p.
    Includes index.
    1. Foster home care—United States. 2. Foster
parents—United States. 3. Social work with children—
United States. I. Title.
HV875.G779   362.7'33'0973   77-521
ISBN 0-87705-281-6

In 1799, a number of Boston women began writing anonymous letters to the *Boston Gazette* following the publication of the story of a young orphan girl who was "destitute, neglected and . . . betrayed." Funds were then raised, the list of donors being headed by Abigail Adams, the First Lady of the Nation. Thus the Boston Female Asylum, the first of the agencies later to become Boston Children's Service Association, came into being.

SOCIAL WORK SERIES

CONTENTS

PREFACE

In 1930, a Children's Charter was created by the representatives to the White House Conference on Children and Youth. It stated that every homeless child had an unshakable right to foster parents and that each was entitled to the love and security that a home provides. Foster home care has grown substantially since then. Most citizens have been comforted by the thought that homeless children in their community are cared for.

Much research over the last years seems to indicate that foster home care is failing its purposes. Nonetheless, necessary changes and improvements in the system have not been forthcoming. The Massachusetts Governor's Commission on Adoption and Foster Care set out to identify some of those problem areas in order to update the processes by which foster children are cared for and to establish a modernized system which would be more responsive to the needs of the children and their families.

Later, the Massachusetts Developmental Disabilities Council provided the funds for the exploration of "Domiciliary Alternatives for the Care of the Developmentally Disabled Child." This allowed for the assessment of quality, extent and scope of foster home services to disabled children in the Commonwealth.

The results of these studies have borne out the impression that our system of caring for children separated from their families is in considerable disarray. The very system which is mandated to provide for the child all too often is unconscionably neglectful. We create the illusion that the child is provided with the required emotional supplies, food and shelter. At the same time, we fail to ever ask whether indeed the objectives are being achieved.

Foster children are, in almost every way, the most disadvantaged people in our society. In spite of this fact, even when it becomes painfully visible, we deny our responsibility and simply wait out the outcry until, once again, the voices have faded into the background. It is not that our social welfare system cannot work, it is that, all too often, our leaders of state lack the moral commitment to act on the pressing issues. Thus, children in foster care remain the "orphans of the living."

In spite of these facts, it is my sincere hope that the experience and findings reported in this volume may provide some impetus and guideline for meaningful changes. Those changes are long overdue.

A.R.G.

ACKNOWLEDGEMENTS

To Judge Edmund V. Keville, then Chairman of the Governor's Commission on Adoption and Foster Care, for his consistent support, wisdom and critical counsel. He was a hard taskmaster.

To Judith Meredith and Elton Klibanoff, staff members of the Commission, for their insights and perseverance.

To Linda Bedford, Research Associate; Rachel Crystal, Barbara Amidon and Ellen Mintzer, Project Assistants, for their immeasurable assistance in collection and processing of data. Without their efforts, this study could not have been completed.

To Thomas Riley, Diane Zagrodny and Carol Trust, social workers on the staff of the Massachusetts Department of Public Welfare, Division of Family and Children's Services, who served major liaison functions over the course of the study, for their consultation and unstinting cooperation.

To Dr. Doris Fraser and Carol Markowitz, of the Massachusetts Bureau of Developmental Disabilities, for their insights, consultation, and support. The Massachusetts Development Disabilities Council provided support for part of this research.

To Steven A. Minter and Martha Davis Dunn, then Commissioner and Assistant Commissioner for Social Services, respectively, of the Massachusetts Department of Public Welfare, for their commitment to children and families and their courage to allow the questions and issues to be raised.

To Charles W. Bates, then Executive Director of Boston Children's Service Association, who steadfastly supported the research program at Boston Children's Service Association and provided counsel, encouragement and enthusiasm throughout his tenure.

To Richard J. Bond, Executive Director, and Dr. Edward T. Heck, Associate Director of Research and Evaluation, Boston Children's Service Association, for their advice, consultation and support.

To Wilhelmina Hollingsworth for her untiring secretarial labors. She has typed so much of this material over the years that she virtually has it memorized!

To the many social workers who carried the cases and provided the data which provided the basis for this study. Their willingness to participate, even in the midst of so many other pressures, is a measure of their commitment to the children in their care.

To the foster parents who quietly go about the work of caring for children so often neglected by the very system designed to provide for them.

Finally, to the children and families. They are the real substance of this report. Would that some day they will live in a more sensitive, conscientious and caring society.

Chapter 1

INTRODUCTION

The unwillingness or inability of parents to maintain responsibility for their children and the subsequent separation of children from families is a familiar problem. Over the years, a variety of mechanisms have been established to provide children with food and shelter. Some of these mechanisms were less than humane, especially by contemporary standards. Recent literature clarifies the fact that too often children are placed in foster care with little planning for their future or protection of their rights. Effective social work and other services are frequently not implemented, and the consequences are that alternatives to separation are not explored. When separation occurs, whether or not it was actually the best plan, the child and family are often not reunited.[1]

Because separating children from their families created so many problems, the Commonwealth of Massachusetts pioneered the foster home care system in the

1860's. At that time, in order to avoid placing children in institutions, the state provided funds for the boarding of children in private homes. During the same period, indenturing was one of the more common means of providing care for homeless children. Massachusetts developed the first program to give indentured children adequate supervision. This program was established because so many children were abused by those to whom they were indentured. Even in the society which did not yet see fit to establish child labor laws, these abuses struck at the sensibilities of many of the populace.

Boston Children's Aid Society (now Boston Children's Service Association) brought about considerable changes in foster home programs. Charles Birtwell, Director of the agency from 1886 to 1911, felt that each child needed to be treated individually to assure that his particular needs were served. Under his leadership, foster parent studies were instituted and each child was supervised while in care. In addition, discreet records began to be kept on each child.

In 1909, President Theodore Roosevelt sponsored the first White House Conference on the Care of Dependent Children. At that time, foster home care was presented as the best way to provide for the child who could not be cared for at home. By 1910, 176,000 children had been removed from or surrendered by their families. That figure was 266,000 children in 1971.[2] An analysis of the statistics shows that both the numbers and the proportions have increased over the years. In 1933, for instance, the rate of placement in foster family care was 2.5 per 1000 children, while the projected rate for 1975 was 3.9 per 1000 children. To a great extent, this is because proportions of children placed in institutions have substantially decreased.[3] These figures nonetheless reinforce the fact that it is not standard practice to explore alternatives to separating children from their families.

The Child Welfare League of America defines foster

family care as a "child welfare service which provides substitute family care for a planned period for a child when his
own family cannot care for him for a temporary extended
period."[4] It is especially important to note that the care is
to be provided for a *planned* period, either temporary or
extended, but it is not meant to be a permanent family.

One of the greatest problems associated with foster
home care is that it seems to have become a program of
permanent care. One study conducted by Maas and Engler
shows that only about 25% of children placed in foster care
ever return to their own homes.[5] Another study by Gambrill and Wiltse showed that even for those children whose
plan called for return to their parents, when followed a year
later, there is less than a 50% chance that these children
were restored to their natural homes.[6] The Jeter Study
discovered that the only plan that public agencies had for
2/3 of the children in their care was to continue their placements.[7] A study of 1,766 children in foster homes in England showed that the average child had been in care for
about 5 years.[8] Of these children, 97% had at least one
living parent but 8% were "never seen."[9]

The Maas and Engler study indicated that once a child
was in care beyond 1 1/2 years, his chances of being
adopted or returned to his biological family decreased.[10]
Commenting on that finding, Kadushin has stated that "the
ties of natural parents to children become attenuated; the
feeling of responsibility for the child not being actively
exercised, atrophies; the parents reorganize their lives in a
way that does not include the child, so that the child's
return would mean disruption of the current situation. All
this encourages separation that is total except in legal
terms."[11]

In part, this situation is probably the result of many of
the parents never receiving professional assistance from
the agency which supervised their child's foster home
placement. The Jeter study, for instance, found that over
1/3 of the parents of children under public agency auspices

were not receiving casework assistance. The same was true
for almost 1/4 of the parents whose children were placed
in private agencies.[12] Another study conducted by Bernice
Boehm found that in a sample of 30 families with children
in foster care, only two were receiving casework services
considered to be adequate. Of the 30 cases, 14 were not
receiving services at all.[13] There was simply no evidence
that either public or private agencies provided the necessary services to reunite a child and family once they had
been separated.

Almost all studies have shown that virtually no services
are available to biological families after a child has been
placed in foster home care. Aggravating the situation is the
fact that most of these families are at high risk to begin with.
Supportive and restitutive services would have to be of the
highest quality to have any substantial effect. These facts
have led agencies to disregard families rather than make
efforts to bring about positive change. A study conducted
in 1960 by the State Charities Aid Association in New York
reported that over 3/4 of the families they studied ". . . had
such a serious degree of social and emotional incompetence as to render them in all probability beyond the hope
of salvage for the particular child."[14] Judgments such as
these were made continually without the benefit of consistent adequate high quality services to test out the tradition
that a child cannot, in fact, be returned to his own home.

Another very serious problem that many studies indicate is that large numbers of children have been operationally abandoned by their parents. Parents place their
children in foster home care under voluntary legal status
but many never see their children again. From a practical
standpoint these parents have permanently surrendered
their children. Yet the parent in this situation maintains
legal rights and never agrees to allow the child to be
adopted. These children are simply maintained by the state
in a sort of "legal limbo."

One general problem in providing foster home care for children is the relationship of the foster parent to the agency. There is a high turnover rate of social workers, particularly in public agencies. The character of foster home care is changing as well. The consequences are that parents are expected to take on considerably more responsibility than they have in the past. The compassion and altruism which initially motivated so many families to accept foster children soon begins to wane and is often replaced by frustration. Adequate financial return will be increasingly necessary in order to sustain foster family care. At the current payment rate, which is often considerably less than $100 per month, many foster parents are actually supporting foster children with their own family income. Since there are indications that foster children are older and more physically and emotionally handicapped than in the past, most foster families will need more than "psychological return" to sustain their involvement.

The Research Problem

Recognizing the importance of the issues above, the Governor of Massachusetts, Francis W. Sargent, established the Governor's Commission on Adoption and Foster Care. The Commission was actually established in August, 1971, with the mandate to:

a. Identify important problems in Massachusetts relating to adoption and foster care
b. Evaluate existing procedures relating to adoption and foster care
c. Make specific recommendations to the Governor and the General Court (of Massachusetts) for changes in the statutes or procedures relating to adoption and foster care

One of the first acts of the Commission was to establish subcommittees. The Subcommittee on Research and Recommendations was assigned the task of providing the Commission with specific data on the children. It became quickly apparent, however, that such data were almost totally lacking. Recognizing that the Commission could not fulfill its function without reliable information, this research project was proposed and funded.

The purpose of this study has been to identify the characteristics and problems of children in foster home care in Massachusetts under public or private auspices. Based upon the findings of this study, recommendations were to be forwarded to the Commission.

Research Methodology

This study was designed as a 1-day survey which attempted to gather data on every child in foster home care in Massachusetts under public or private auspices on November 18, 1971. In addition, data were obtained from a random sample of biological parents and a random sample of foster parents.

The particular target date was chosen because that was the most current listing of children in foster home care under the auspices of the Massachusetts Department of Public Welfare. That listing had to be obtained from the Accounting Office of the Department since the listing used by the Division of Family and Children's Services, the arm of the organization responsible for foster children, was at least 3 months out of date. Master lists were requested from all private agencies licensed to provide foster home care in the state.

Early in the process, meetings with the social work staff were held in each of the Department's regions. There were two additional meetings with representatives of the private agencies.

Questionnaires were used to collect information on each child. As the master lists were received, the child's name and/or agency identification number was placed on the questionnaire. It was then forwarded to the agency or office of the Department reponsible for that child's supervision with instructions for it to be completed by the social worker most immediately responsible for the child's supervision. If the case was uncovered, it was to be completed by the supervisor or his designee.

The second and third phases of the study were to gather data from biological and foster parents via two separate research instruments. The parents were selected by random process.

The fourth phase of the study was to collect information from the Department and private agencies regarding policies, procedures and statistics for their foster home care programs.

Questionnaires completed by social workers were returned to the project at the rate of 98.8% of the 5,933 children in foster home care on November 18, 1971 in Massachusetts. Data are available on 5,862. This attests to the remarkable cooperation and concern of a great many people in the conduct of this study.

To test for reliability, 57 cases were selected at random. Project staff were assigned to complete their questionnaires on each, and the responses were compared to those of the social worker who completed the original. In turn, 30 items not relying solely on the social workers' judgment were randomly selected for statistical comparison.[15] The agreement was remarkably high. Of the 30 items, 18 had over 90% agreement and 9 were between 80 and 90%. Only 3 items were below 80%.

Each child's questionnaire was returned to the Department of Public Welfare regional agencies and private agencies to be included in the child's permanent record. In that way, the data collected served the purpose of a synopsis of the case.

Foster Home Care Policies And Statistics—Private Agencies

Twenty-seven private agencies provided the information requested by the Project staff. Five agencies failed to respond. The information reflected below is based on agency responses for early 1972.

None of the agencies specified the criteria which were utilized to distinguish foster parents for children with special needs. One-third of the agencies provide no training for the foster parent, another third offered general orientation. The remainder offered "extra" training, none of which was identified, for foster parents designated as "professional."

In most agencies the caseworker assumes the responsibility for the foster home. Only two agencies indicated that they utilize a foster home supervisor/coordinator. Every agency indicated that contact with the foster home was at least on a monthly basis. However, the validity of that statement was never tested.

With regard to costs, the weekly fee charged to a parent or guardian of a child is dependent upon the family's ability to pay. When specific fees were listed, they were almost always equal to the foster parent payment per child per week. At that time, the weekly payment to the foster parents ranged from $12 to $40 and was usually between $15 and $25. Most agencies were unable to designate their actual costs since their accounting programs were not geared to costing out programs and services. The agencies which do have the capability indicated that the actual costs of foster home care exceed the payment due the foster parent by at least $30 to $35 a week.

Table 1.1 provides a statistical summary of private agency foster home care as of April 1, 1972, in Massachusetts.

The private agencies overwhelmingly designated their

foster homes as temporary. To a great extent, this is due to the fact that so many are for infants only.

Private agencies showed a considerable number of unfilled spaces. Half of these were for infants, but at least 85 were for children with special needs or older children. Especially interesting is the fact that 8 adolescents were waiting to be placed on April 1, 1972, while there were 31 vacancies in adolescent homes, and an additional 26 waiting for approval. It is suspected that the private agencies were delaying the actual placement until the Department of Public Welfare assured reimbursement under purchase-of-service agreements.

Finally, it can be seen from Table 1.1 that the private agencies average two or less children in a foster home.

FOSTER HOME CARE POLICIES AND STATISTICS— DEPARTMENT OF PUBLIC WELFARE

Comparable figures to those in Table 1.1 could not be obtained for the Massachusetts Department of Public Welfare, Division of Family and Children's Services, since the data could only be obtained from two of the regional offices. The figures from these two offices, however, indicated that 927 homes were being supervised and they contained 1,436 children. One hundred and eight foster families were waiting for approval and no children were waiting for placement. The two offices indicated that they had at least 170 spaces for additional children. This is in spite of the fact that, as can be seen in following sections of this report, 20% of the Division's homes were overcrowded according to its own standards.

The questionnaire completed by the administration of the Division of Family and Children's Services did not indicate that there is any formal criteria for differentiating foster homes for children of special needs.

TABLE 1.1 Summary of Private Agency Foster Home Care Statistics

Number of	Type of Home				
	General	Infant	Adolescent	Special Medical	Total
homes agency is supervising	152	260	89	18	519
approved spaces in these homes	261	322	138	18	739
children in these homes	133	181	110	20	444
homes designated for temporary placement	101	217	21	9	348
homes designated for permanent placements	47	48	63	1	159

homes designated as temporary and permanent	0	1	2	0	3
children waiting to be placed	1	4	8	0	13
spaces available but not being used	56	137	31	1	225
homes agency closed in past year	7	48	4	2	61
professional foster homes	0	0	2	10	12
homes awaiting approval	12	16	26	1	55

The Division's Standards state that "the agency, as legal or temporary guardian, retains the principal responsibility for the child. Let it be noted that although work with foster parents around a particular child in placement is the responsibility of that child's worker . . . the development of the foster home should not be dependent upon the child or children's social worker, but rather be handled within the agency structure." This seems to focus more on the responsibility for the foster home than the foster child. Yet nowhere else in the Standards is responsibility for the child more explicitly defined. Though the Division's administration indicated that "the placement worker carries main responsibility for the foster child," over 1/3 of the children have no staff member assigned to his case.

NOTES

1. See for example: David Fanshel, "The Exit of Children from Foster Care: An Interim Research Report," *Child Welfare*, Vol. 50 (5) (February, 1971), pp. 65–81; Henry Maas and Richard Engler, *Children in Need of Parents* (New York: Columbia University Press, 1959); David Fanshel and Eugene B. Shinn, *Dollars and Sense in the Foster Care of Children* (New York: Child Welfare League of America, Inc., 1972); *Children Waiting* (Sacramento: State Social Welfare, Board of California, 1972); Kermit T. Wiltse and Eileen Gambrill, "Foster Care, 1973: A Reappraisal," *Public Welfare*, Volume 32 (1) (Winter, 1974), pp. 7–15; and Eileen D. Gambrill and Kermit T. Wiltse, "Foster Care: Planned and Actualities," *Public Welfare*, Volume 32 (2) (Spring, 1974), pp. 12–21.

2. *Children served by public welfare agencies and voluntary child welfare agencies and institutions, March, 1971* (U. S. Department of Health, Education, and Welfare), National Center for Social Statistics, 1973.

3. Alfred Kadushin, *Child Welfare Services* (New York: Macmillan Co., 1974), page 363.

4. *Standards for Foster Family Care* (New York: Child Welfare League of America, Inc., In press).

5. Maas and Engler, *Op. cit.*

6. Gambrill and Wiltse, *Op. cit.*

7. Helen R. Jeter, *Children, Problems and Services in Child Welfare Programs* (Washington, D.C.: U. S. Government Printing Office, 1963), page 87.

8. P. G. Gray and E. A. Parr, *Children in Care and the Recruitment of Foster Parents* (London: Social Survey, 1957), page 10.

9. *Ibid.,* page 23.

10. Maas and Engler, *Op. cit.,* page 351.

11. Kadushin, *Op. cit.,* page 412.

12. Jeter, *Op. cit.,* pp. 85–86.

13. Bernice Boehm, *Deterrents to the Adoption of Children in Foster Care* (New York: Child Welfare League of America, Inc., 1958), page 18.

14. *Adoptability—A Study of 100 Children in Foster Home Care* (New York: State Charities Aid Association, Child Adoption Service, 1960), page 27.

15. Percentage agreement scores were computed in the traditional fashion: percentage agreement equals 2 (number of agreements) over total number of observations.

Chapter 2

THE CHILDREN

Information obtained on children in foster home care was gathered by means of a questionnaire completed by the social worker assigned to the child's case. A great number of cases in the public sector, i.e., the Department of Public Welfare, were uncovered. In most instances, a social worker was assigned by the Department to review the record and provide the necessary data.

The total number of children in foster home care in the Commonwealth of Massachusetts on November 18, 1971, was 5,933. Data were available for 5,862 of these children. There were 71 cases missing because 22 questionnaires were returned too late to be included, 11 records were reported as missing from the Department of Public Welfare District Office, 15 questionnaires were reported as completed but never received at the Research Center, and 23 were never received at the Research Center for reasons unknown to the staff.

IDENTIFYING INFORMATION

One of the most important findings is that foster home care is almost entirely a public function. Of the 5,862 cases, 5,327 (91%) were in the care of the Massachusetts Department of Public Welfare, Division of Family and Children's Services. (Of particular import is the fact that approximately 32% of those cases are uncovered, i.e., have no social worker assigned. There is no indication that this situation has changed substantially since the publication of the original report.)

Furthermore, the 507 children in the care of private agencies 332 (67%) were supported by the Commonwealth through purchase-of-service agreements between the Department and the private social agency. Less than 2-2.5% of all children in foster home care were in placements which were financially independent of the state.

Regarding general financial support, only 90 children (1.5%) were fully supported by the biological parents, and an additional 654 (11.2%) were partially supported. Less than 10% of the children received any outside financial assistance from programs such as Veteran's Benefits, private insurance carriers, or Social Security. There are undoubtedly many more children in care who could be at least partially supported by these sources. The state, however, has no mechanism for billing or tracking payments. Social workers are seldom aware of this issue and rarely discuss financial arrangements for the child beyond family income level. So long as information gathering at the point of intake is not standardized, outside resources will probably not be tapped to the extent to which they should be. On the other hand, even if data on these resources were available, there are not the personnel to implement collection procedures for them.

Table 2.1 presents the data relating to the children's age. The average age of a child in foster home care in 1971 was approximately 10.5 years. Slightly less than 7% of the children (40.6) were less than 1 year old, and approximately 24% (1,419) were under the age of 5. Approximately 28.5% (1,681) were between 5 and 10 years old. A similar number, 1,659 were between 11 and 15 years old. Finally, slightly less than 19% of the youths (1,101) were between the ages of 16 and 21.

The mean, median, and modal age of children in foster home care was 10 years old. Over 62% of the children were between the ages of 5 and 15. With respect to sex, there is a relatively even split; 46.6% of the children were female and 52.3% male. The sex of slightly less than 2% of the population was unknown due to blanks left on the questionnaires.

Table 2.2 shows that when age and sex are cross-tabulated, the proportion of males in each age group is generally similar to the proportion of females. It is notable, however, that in the older age groups the proportion of girls is slightly higher. This observation implies that given the significant changes in social attitudes about behavioral differences among males and females, the future will probably find more girls than boys in foster home care. If there are slightly more older girls than older boys in foster home care at present, the assumption is that as social institutions are confronted with more aggressive female behavior and are either unable or unwilling to contend with it, the number of girls in care will increase. This outcome will presumably shift the balance. Even given that this increasing aggressiveness among girls is probably more appropriate than not, inability of our institutions to cope with it will probably keep them from responding appropriately. This projection has been at least partially validated by the observation of increasing numbers of females in care between 1971 when these data were originally collected and 1974.

Table 2.3 presents the data pertaining to racial/ethnic identification.

TABLE 2.1   Ages of Children in Foster Home Care

Age	N	%
Under 1 month	195	3.3
1 to 6 months	142	2.4
6 to 11 months	69	1.2
1 year old	206	3.5
2 years old	245	4.2
3 years old	268	4.6
4 years old	294	5.0
5 years old	328	5.6
6 years old	341	5.8
7 years old	323	5.5
8 years old	350	6.0
9 years old	339	5.8
10 years old	368	6.3
11 years old	314	5.4
12 years old	339	5.8
13 years old	305	5.2
14 years old	333	5.7

15 years old	310	5.3
16 years old	292	5.0
17 years old	227	3.9
18 years old	136	2.3
19 years old	92	1.6
20 years old	43	0.6
21 years old	0	0.0
22 years old	1	0.0
Don't know	2	0.0
Total	5,862	100.0%

The 1970 Census determined that blacks make up 3% of the population in Massachusetts and the percentage of persons of Spanish-speaking descent is slightly more than 1. It is generally presumed, and the data in Chapter 3 confirm, that foster home care is a program primarily utilized by the poor and near-poor. Therefore, the figures in Table 2.3 are probably consistent with expectations.

The religious distribution of the foster children are consistent with expectations. Since it is illegal to ask about religious affiliation in census data, one can only compare these data with estimates. As can be seen from Table 2.4, the largest proportion of the youth are Catholic, with Protestants running second. As with many other such studies, the number of Jewish children in foster home care is well below their proportion in the population at large.

TABLE 2.2 Age and Sex of Children in Foster Home Care

Age	Sex					Total	
	Females		Males				
	N*	%**	N*	%**		N*	%**
Less than 1 year	160	52.8 (5.9)	143	47.2 (4.7)		303	100.0% (5.3)
1 to 5 years	601	45.7 (22.3)	713	54.3 (23.5)		1,314	100.0% (22.9)
6 to 10 years	1,053	44.8 (39.1)	1,296	55.2 (42.7)		2,349	100.0% (41.0)

11 to 15 years	597	48.1 (22.2)	644	51.9 (21.2)	1,241	100.0% (21.7)
Over 15 years	282	54.1 (10.5)	239	45.9 (7.9)	521	100.0% (9.1)
Total	2,693	47.0 (100.0%)	3,035	53.0 (100.0%)	5,728	100.0% (100.0%)

$x^2 = 20.62$ df=4   p= <.001

*134 cases were rejected for lack of specific information
**figures in parentheses refer to column percentages

TABLE 2.3   Racial/Ethnic Identification of Children in Foster Home Care

Race/Ethnic I.D.	N	%
White	4,537	77.3
Black	866	14.8
Interracial B/W	186	3.2
Spanish-speaking	103	1.8
Interracial other	98	1.7
American Indian	28	.5
Oriental	1	.0
Other	20	.3
Don't know	23	.4
Total	5,862	100.0%

With respect to the legal status of children in foster home care, it can be seen from Table 2.5 that over 53% of the children have been placed in a foster home on voluntary status. The Federal Government reimburses a state for 75% of the costs of care if the child was eligible for AFDC and was placed through judicial determination. Since the typical child remains in a foster home for a considerable period of time, the Commonwealth of Massachusetts may be losing substantial Federal funds by failing to design and implement a system of entry into foster home care through a process involving judicial decision.

TABLE 2.4   Religion of Children in Foster Home Care

Religion	N	%
Catholic	3,500	59.7
Protestant	2,057	35.1
Jewish	43	.7
Other	47	.8
None	78	1.3
Don't know	137	2.4
Total	5,862	100.0%

The data in Table 2.5 describe the legal status of children in foster home care and show the proportions of children in each status. One of the findings of the research staff when collecting these data, was that more than half of the fathers were often not involved in the placement process. For example, they were neither signatories to the voluntary placement nor present for the court proceedings. This situation was discussed with the Department and it was stated that unless the father of the child is living in the home at the time of the foster home placement, there is no attempt to involve him in the legal process. Even if there is no legal separation or divorce, no effort is made to obtain signatures from fathers. This is true for voluntary placements as well as those which occur through judicial determination. Given the United States Supreme Court decision (Stanley vs. Illinois), the question must be raised as to what the Constitution requires regarding the father's consent for foster home placement of his child.

TABLE 2.5 Legal Status of Children in Foster Home Care

Legal Status	N	%
Voluntary (private)	453	7.7
Voluntary (public)	2,655	45.4
Child of incarcerated mother	64	1.1
Temporary custody probate court	247	4.2
Permanent custody probate court	155	2.6
Permanent custody probate court with adoption release	53	0.9
Temporary custody district court	395	6.7
Permanent custody district court	1,274	21.7
Permanent custody district court with adoption release	85	1.5
Hearing pending	87	1.5
Appeal pending	42	0.7
Other	325	5.5
Unknown	27	0.5
Total	5,862	100.0%

The data in Table 2.5 indicate that 64% of the children in foster home care are placed on either a voluntary or temporary basis. This implies that almost 2/3 of these children should, theoretically, be discharged to their own families at some not too distant future time. However, the actual length of time which a child is in care is another matter, as will be seen in later sections. Voluntary placement seems to presume temporary status, and temporary status is obviously meant to reflect time limitation. Therefore we must ask whether separation of a child from his family for 2 to 6 years or more can, in fact, be considered temporary.

The truth of the matter is that a large proportion of parents are actually surrendering their child when they place the child in foster home care. Our social values make it extremely difficult for someone to simply admit at the outset that they are not interested in maintaining custody of their offspring. There are no clear characteristics to differentiate those parents who are really surrendering their child from those who need their child temporarily cared for. There must be, however, an explicit policy promulgated which will identify the foster child who has been operationally abandoned, i.e., voluntarily placed in foster home care but with virtually no parent-child contact. Massachusetts law already states that a child who has not had any parental contact for one year or more can be released for adoption if the Department petitions for such action. But as with so many other issues, the Department does not have the personnel with the skill necessary to develop a case tracking system to assure such identification and consequent action. So there remain hundreds of children deprived of permanent families.

Another method of handling this problem could be by actually contracting with a biological parent for foster home care of a child. The contract would then specify the length of time the child is placed for and the frequency with which the parent agrees to visit. Among the responsibilities the parent might carry are taking the child to the physician for an annual physical examination and attending P.T.A. functions. The social worker assigned to the family, then, would have criteria for parental involvement and would know quickly when and if a parent ceases to maintain interest in the child. In the event that occurs, the social worker can act swiftly to either help resolve the problems which keep the parent from following through or to seek the child's release for adoption. This approach, however, presumes that the Department could have the personnel it needs to monitor each case.

THE PLACEMENT

A study conducted in New York City in 1965,[1] established five main reasons for placement of children in foster home care. They were: 1) physical illness or incapacity of the child-caring person[2] (32%)[3]; 2) mental illness of the mother (13%); 3) severe neglect or abuse (10%); 4) personality or emotional problems of the child (8%); 5) other family problems including unwillingness or inability to continue care, children left or deserted, parental incompetence, and conflicts or arrest (37%).

There are dramatic differences in the distribution of reasons for placement when the data from the Jenkins and Sauber study in New York City are compared with these. The most glaring difference is the one related to mental illness. In New York City, 13% of the placements were accounted for by that reason, compared to 23% of the foster home case placements in Massachusetts.

There are two possible explanations for this finding. Together they indicate that the provision of mental health services in Massachusetts is significantly less than optimal. First, the Department of Mental Health has not provided sufficient resources for community-based, out-patient treatment programs. Waiting lists are not uncommon and, even when patients are seen, they are often terminated prematurely due to short staff and caseload pressures. Second, only limited mental health services are provided under the provisions of Title XIX (Medicaid). (This situation relates more directly to the Department of Public Welfare.) There is no way to estimate how many of the 1,859 children placed in foster home care as a result of their parent's mental illness might not have needed placement if appropriate community-based treatment services were available.

Recent studies have shown that foster home care placements can be substantially reduced if viable options are available to the social workers and families. It can be seen, for instance that 2,520 children originally entered foster home care because one or both of their parents were mentally or physically ill. Out of this number, one can only guess how many children could have avoided placement if adequate homemaker services, for instance, had been available on an immediate and 24-hour basis.

More than 2/3 of the children were living with one or both parents just prior to their placement in foster home care. Table 2.7 presents the distribution of those data.

The referral for foster home care in almost half of the cases comes from a social agency. About 25% of the referrals are directly from the parent of the child to the Department of Public Welfare without any intermediary. Slightly less than 18% of the referrals were from the courts.

On the average, once a child has been referred and placed in foster home care, he will remain there for more than 5 years. Placement under the auspices of the agency which currently supervises his placement averages slightly less than 4 years and 10 months. The minimal disparity between those figures shows that most foster home care placements are single agency phenomena. For example, the agency which first takes responsibility for a child's fos-

TABLE 2.6 Reasons for Placement of Children in Foster Home Care*

Reason	N	%
Mental illness of parent	1,859	23.0
Neglect, abuse or inadequate home	1,099	13.6
Divorce or desertion of parent(s)	771	9.5
Abandonment	686	8.5
Physical illness of parent	661	8.2
Mother deciding to keep or surrender child for adoption	505	6.2
Death of parent(s)	367	4.5
Parent(s) in jail	305	3.8
Foster home placement as part of child's treatment for emotional disturbance	289	3.5

Mother hospitalized or bedridden	167	2.1
Alcoholism or other addiction of parent	131	1.6
Referral from juvenile court after committing offense	128	1.6
Child ran away from home	121	1.5
Awaiting adoption (child of unmarried mother)	49	0.6
Child awaiting institutional placement for treatment of emotional disturbance	29	0.4
Other and don't know	917	11.4
Total	8,084	100.0%

*There were 5,862 children in foster home care on November 18, 1971. Some of these children entered placement for more than one reason and the records do not indicate which is primary. The data in Table 11-6, therefore, refer to reasons rather than children.

TABLE 2.7   Residence of Children in Foster Home Care Prior to Placement

Living With	N	%
Mother alone	2,266	38.8
Both parents	1,201	20.4
Infant placement	571	9.7
Father alone	537	9.2
Other relatives	497	8.5
Institution	276	4.7
Guardian	52	.9
Other	331	5.6
Don't know	131	2.2
Total	5,862	100.0%

ter care is the one which maintains it. About 6% of the children had been previously placed with another agency.

Approximately 16% of the children have previously been in foster home care. Of those 943 children, almost 3/4 (73.5%) had been placed once before, 16% had been placed twice, 6.4% are in their fourth placement and 4.2% have been placed more than four times. There was not as much movement from one foster home to another as was originally expected. More than half the children have never left the foster home in which they were originally placed.

Table 2.8 shows that the most typical length of placement is between 1 and 2 years. Fifty-six percent of the youths have been in placement for anywhere from 1 to 7 years.

The standard deviation for the length of time that a child is in foster home care under the auspices of the present placement agency is 21.39 months. Approximately 68% of the children have been in foster home care for between slightly more than 4 years and slightly less than 7 years and 7 months. Since the average age of a child in foster home care is 10.5 years, it is probable that many children have spent a major portion of their lives separated from their biological parents.

Less than 3% of the children coming into care will be discharged in less than 2 years and 4 months. On the other end of the scale, an equal number of children will be in care for at least 9 years and 4 months.

At the time of initial entry into foster home care, almost 1/2 of the children (49.4%) are stated to be entering care for some specified length of time. Almost 1/3 of those children (31.4%) even had a specific discharge date attached to their placement. However, 83% of the children have never been returned to their biological parents, not even for a trial period.

Adoption Potential

Over the last few years, the number of children available for adoption, especially the number of white infants, has dropped. A diversity of reasons explain this situation. More single mothers tend to keep their babies rather than give them up for adoption. Abortion is more accessible. Contraceptive measures are utilized more often.

The assumption has been that the children in foster

TABLE 2.8   Length of Time That Child Has Been in Foster Home Care*

Length of Time	N	%
Under 1 month	70	1.2
2 to 6 months	549	9.5
7 to 11 months	458	7.9
1 year	809	14.1
2 years	606	10.5
3 years	539	9.3
4 years	434	7.5
5 years	468	8.1
6 years	374	6.5
7 years	262	4.5
8 years	262	4.5
9 years	231	4.0
10 years	172	3.0
11 years	144	2.5
12 years	105	1.8
13 years	97	1.7
14 years	67	1.2

15 years	49	0.8
16 years	43	0.7
17 years	20	0.3
18 years	19	0.3
19 years	2	0.0
20 years	7	0.1
21 years	0	0.0
Total	5,787**	100.0%

*One year represents an interval of 1 year but less than 2 years, 2 years represents an interval of 2 years but less than 3 years, etc.
**Information was unavailable on 75 children.

home care are usually not able to be adopted either because their parents maintain interest or some other similar reason. Though one frequently hears that these children are not candidates for adoption, this study appears to find that such a statement is generally inaccurate.

Table 2.9 presents the data provided by the social workers when asked about whether or not adoption had been considered for the child. Of particular interest is that less than 30% of the children have parents who continue to show interest in them. It may be remembered from an earlier section, for instance, that only 136 children entered placement with a legal status freeing them for adoption.

The social workers were asked about the frequency of parent contact with the child. The statistics remain consis-

TABLE 2.9 Adoption Status of Children in Foster Home Care

Adoption Status	N	%
Child is presently considered to be adoptable*	1,857	31.8
Child not presently considered to be adoptable because:		
1. Natural parents are interested	1,740	29.7
2. Child is too old	676	11.5
3. Child has made good adjustment to foster home	375	6.4
4. Child's handicap is too severe	288	4.9
5. Child does not want to be adopted	180	3.1
6. Child's siblings are also in care and adoption of child would be too difficult for them to adjust to	147	2.5
7. Foster parents would like to adopt him but do not have enough personal income to afford another child	127	2.2
8. Child is in foster home care for treatment of emotional disturbance	79	1.3

9.	Foster parents would like to adopt him but are concerned about other children in their home	16	0.3
10.	Adoption procedure is too involved	13	0.2
11.	Other	228	3.9
12.	Don't know	136	2.2
	Total	5,862	100.0%

*It should be understood that these children are considered to be adoptable by the social worker providing data on their cases but that does not necessarily mean that the child is actually free for adoption, i.e., has obtained releases, etc.

---

tent on this point. It was found that less than 30% of the children had seen one of their parents in a given 3 month period. Approximately 38% had seen their parent(s) some time within the last 6 months. The remaining children had no substantive parental contact.

Table 2.10, however, provides additional information regarding this point. When the children considered are only those who are categorized as nonadoptable because their parents remain interested in them, parental visitation, as an indicator of interest, does not seem to be directly related.

As can be seen, over 11% of the biological parents or guardians have not seen their child in foster home care for at least 6 months. Yet, the social workers have still designated the child as unadoptable because of parental interest.

TABLE 2.10   Frequency of Visitation of Children in Foster Home Care by Biological Parent(s) or Guardian

Approximate Frequency of Visits in 6 Month Period	N	%
Once a week or more	216	12.4
Twice a month	282	16.2
Once a month	351	20.2
Once every 2 months	129	7.4
Once every 3 months	150	8.6
Once in 6 months	175	10.1
Never in 6 months	194	11.1
Don't know	243	14.0
Total	1,740	100.0%

An additional 10% of the children so designated have seen their parents or guardians once in a six month period. Perhaps even of greater concern is the fact that in 14% of the cases, the child has been designated as unadoptable when the social worker knows nothing of the frequency of contact. There are almost as many parents who have not seen their child for at least 6 months as there are parents who see their child twice a month or more. And there are just as many instances where the social worker does not know about the frequency of biological parent or guardian and child contact. Nonetheless, all of these children are considered to be unadoptable due to parental interest. Massachusetts laws (G.L., ch. 210, s. 3) state that parental rights can be abrogated and the child can be freed for adoption in the event that there is no child-parent contact for 12 months or more. There seems to be a lack of mechanisms which would serve to monitor this, however, and the consequence is that even though the statute exists, there is a general inability or unwillingness to utilize it. This would appear to be the case for two reasons. First, the Department does not have enough personnel to attend to all of the cases as they should be. Secondly, the Department lacks the appropriate case information systems which would be necessary for adequate monitoring.

The above clearly implies that policies defining unadoptability by virtue of parental interest must be clearly and operationally established. In addition, an agency must have the staff and technological capacity to be able to assure compliance with that policy.

Table 2.9 also indicates that 375 children are not considered adoptable when they have adjusted well to foster home care. It is probably true that these children are in relatively good emotional health. They would, undoubtedly, adjust just as well to an adoptive home. But since they are not causing any problems at present, it is easier, given such great caseload pressures, to maintain the status quo. The consequences are, of course, that the child is deprived of permanent legal and emotional stability.

Table 2.9 shows that there are 127 children who remain in foster home care with foster parents who would like to adopt them, but lack sufficient family income to support another child. The social workers were asked whether or not a subsidized adoption program might have some bearing on that child's status. Table 2.11 presents a cross-tabulation of those children by the response of the social workers.

Table 2.11 shows that the social workers believe that more than 3/4 of the children whose foster parents would like to adopt them but have insufficient funds to do so,

TABLE 2.11 Children Considered to Be Unadoptable Because Foster Parents Have Insufficient Funds by Subsidized Adoption Program

Would plans for adoption be affected if Massachusetts had subsidized adoptions?	Is child considered to be unadoptable because his foster parents lack the income to adopt him?			
	Yes		No	
	N	%	N	%
Yes	96	77.4	603	11.0
No	16	12.9	3,765	68.4
Don't know	12	9.7	1,138	20.6
Total	124	100.0%	5,506	100.0%

$x^2 = 494.27$ df=2   p=<.001

would probably be adopted if Massachusetts had a subsidized adoption program. Subsequently, early in 1972, a subsidized adoption program was passed by the Massachusetts Legislature. However, more than a year later only three of the children had in fact been adopted under this program. Most of the children had not been referred to the unit which arranges such subsidy. Once again, this shows how the fate of a child depends upon whether or not a social worker decides the plan is appropriate and then finally implements it.

It would seem that the social workers are either not aware of the program or simply fail to make the referrals to the Adoption Placement Unit. If the cases are uncovered, there are no social workers to refer them. The result of this is that many of these children continue to be deprived of permanent families.

This situation was discussed with the personnel of the Massachusetts Department of Public Welfare's Adoption Placement Unit (A.P.U.). They pointed out that many foster parents become extremely ambivalent about a prospective adoption as they come closer to it. The Department, however, does not have the personnel to deal with that ambivalence and so many foster parents simply withdraw. On a more empirical plane, the A.P.U. personnel stated that many foster parents simply do not trust the program. Many have withdrawn as prospective adoptive parents because they were afraid that the legislature would stop appropriating funds after the adoption had gone through. The result would be serious financial difficulties for the family.

Table 2.9 also shows that 676 children are considered to be unadoptable because they are too old. In addition, 288 children are designated as too handicapped to be adoptable. These designations are maintained in spite of the fact that adoption of the older child and the handicapped child have become almost commonplace over the last few years.

Table 2.12 addresses the relationship between age and unadoptability. Of the children who are considered to be unadoptable, 17% are 12 years old or less. It appears that due to the lack of explicit policy and mechanisms for assuring compliance, a faulty judgment on the part of some social workers prevents at least some of these children from being adopted. Even more blatant are the decisions that 13 children who are 4 years old or younger are "too old." The obvious solution to this problem is to generate a policy

TABLE 2.12   Age of Children in Foster Home Care Designated as "Too Old" to Be Adoptable

Age	N	%
5 years or less	13	1.9
6 through 10 years	39	5.8
11 years	25	3.7
12 years	39	5.8
13 years	51	7.5
14 years	77	11.4
15 years	99	14.6
16 years	104	15.4
17 years	98	14.5
18 years	131	19.4
Total	676	100.0%

which requires all children, in spite of age, handicaps, etc., to be considered to be potential for adoption and to be referred to the proper unit.

Given what has been stated about adoption, the social work staff were asked about their anticipation of legal adoption for the child. In spite of the fact that 1,857 children were considered to be adoptable, as was seen in Table 2.9, only 1,364, or 73.5% are actually considered by the social workers as children who will probably be adopted. The social worker assigned to the case could only specify a date for adoption in about 16% of the cases. Although almost 3/4 of the children were viewed as ultimately being placed for adoption, the social worker did not know when that might come about. Eleven percent of those children for whom the social workers anticipated legal adoption had not yet been referred to the Adoption Placement Unit.

There are many reasons which could explain why these discrepancies in practice seem to be occurring, such as staff shortages and consequent case overloads, or policies regarding uncovered cases. More likely is the fact that the Department's Division of Family and Child Services had never promulgated and implemented an explicit set of policies regarding the handling of cases. There are no specified mechanisms whereby a child designated as adoptable is referred to the Adoption Placement Unit (A.P.U.), so that some opportunity for consideration of adoption actually exists. From the other end, some children have been reported as referred to the A.P.U. but not accepted because the A.P.U. staff felt that the child was inappropriate. The referral to the A.P.U. is almost a matter of chance. So long as it remains a function of the worker who has the knowledge to know how to make the referral, to think about it and act on it, this situation will probably endure. There should be a specific mechanism for automatic referral to the A.P.U. or some similar unit, of every child who could conceivably be adopted, whether or not, at that point, they are legally free. The adoption unit could then assume the responsibility of arranging for those children not yet legally freed to obtain such status. The Department can set standards for adoptability according to operational criteria. An automatic case information system could then easily assure that those policies are adhered to unless the appropriate personnel decide upon specific exceptions.

The social workers were asked to indicate the length of time which has elapsed since the adoption process should have been started for the child. The responses indicate that of the 1,857 children who were designated as adoptable, 1,571 should have had the process begin before it actually did. Table 2.13 indicates how those figures distribute. It can be seen from Table 2.13 that more than 42% of the children could have had the adoption process started for them more than a year before these data were collected. It is obvious that some delays, even in the best of settings, will occur as a matter of course. It is rather difficult, however, to justify the fact that the 667 children have been held in foster home care when they may have been living with families of their own but for the lack of personnel or resources which are needed to bring that about. Specifically, 24% of the delays have been caused by staff shortages, 18% because of the resistance of biological parents, 7% because judicial processes abrogating parental rights are being contested, 8% due to the child's physical handicaps, 6% due to the child's emotional handicap, 3% because information on the child is incomplete, and 34% for a variety of other reasons.

Of the 5,862 children in foster home care in Massachusetts, 775 (13.2%) are free for adoption. Of that number, 28% have been free for adoption up to 1 year, 16% between 1 and 2 years, 22% from 2 through 5 years, and 33% over 5 years. Almost 3/4 of these children are 10 years old or less; 98 of them are 1 year old or less. The specific problem is that almost every child who has been released

**TABLE 2.13   Length of Time Which Has Elapsed
Since Adoption Process Should Have Begun for
Children in Foster Home Care**

Time Elapsed	N	%
1 month or less	156	9.9
2 months	128	8.1
3 to 6 months	291	18.5
7 to 9 months	138	8.8
10 to 12 months	191	12.2
1 to 2 years	227	14.4
More than 2 years	440	28.1
Total	1,571	100.0%

for adoption but remains in foster home care is handi-capped in some way. There are 38% who are emotionally disturbed, 14% who have some specific medical problem, almost 10% with some speech defect, and another 10% who have a handicap related to leg/foot use.

These facts would seem to indicate that, given the present system, adoption of the child with special problems is highly unlikely unless special mechanisms are instituted. The Department has the capacity to underwrite medical costs after adoption or to otherwise financially assist a pro-spective adoptive parent. The Department's personnel, however, do not seem to be aware of this and, as a consequence, some of these children are held in foster home care unnecessarily.

A major challenge which the state has failed to meet is that of freeing the many remaining children in foster homes who could otherwise qualify for adoption. In most cases, this must be done through a decree of the Probate court, which does not require the consent of the biological parents to the child's adoption. This procedure is accomplished by the Department's legal staff filing in the court a petition known in Massachusetts as a 210 Petition. The procedure is, of course, unnecessary when the parent's release is obtained through voluntary surrender.

The social workers were asked to indicate whether or not the legal releases for adoption of those children previously classified as adoptable would be obtained through a 210 petition. Their responses showed that in slightly less than 1/2 the cases (48.6%) release for adoption would be through a 210 and in about 1/4 of the cases (26.7%) release will be procured through voluntary surrender. The staff did not know how the releases would be obtained in the remaining cases, but it is a fair assumption that the 210 petition would be needed in most of these cases as well.

A major dilemma in this process is that in 37.6% of the cases, the petition had not yet been filed in court. What appeared to be more critical is that almost 1/2 (46.9%) had been filed more than a year prior to the date of this study without having been brought to trial.

A study of the docket in the Suffolk Probate Court (covering Boston and much of its environs) in February, 1972, revealed that petitions for 48 children filed by the Department had been on file without being marked for trial for a period of 1 to more than 3 years. This means that during that time the attorney for the State had not requested that the actual hearing be scheduled. The significance of this fact becomes clear when one considers the valuable time lost in the lives of these children, many of whom might have been adopted in the interim.

Until early 1972, the Massachusetts Department of Public Welfare had in effect a one-man legal staff to try these cases for the entire state. All of the cases by statute had to be brought in the Suffolk County Probate Court. The staff was and to a great extent still is critically under-manned. If the State is to fulfill its obligation to free for adoption the several hundred children abandoned by their own families and now entrenched in foster care, it is vital that the legal staff be adequate and efficient to keep these cases moving.

One last point regarding the possible adoption of children is the small proportion who have been referred to the Massachusetts Adoption Resource Exchange (MARE) and/or the Adoption Resource Exchange of America (ARENA). It was shown in Table 2.9 that 964 children are not considered to be adoptable because they are either "too old" or because the handicap is too severe. The data from this study indicate that 183 children have been referred to MARE or ARENA. Assuming that all of the 183 referred are part of the group of 964, which is doubtful, only 19% are in the MARE or ARENA files. This is in spite of the fact that the Commonwealth underwrites MARE specifically to assist in the adoption of hard-to-place children and they have been quite successful to date.

STAFFING ISSUES

A number of studies have been published within the last dozen years or so which document an annual staff attrition rate of 30 to 40% in Departments of Public Welfare. Massachusetts loses almost 1/3 of its public welfare personnel each year. The effect is that, to a great extent, casework personnel are not in the employ of the Department of Public Welfare long enough to assure any real continuity of service for children in foster home care.

Complicating this issue was the fact that the Division of Family and Children's Services decentralized at about the same time that this study was conducted. The result was that 902 cases (15.4%) had been transferred to new social workers.

Given these considerations, it was discovered that only about 16% of the cases had been in the same social worker's caseload for more than 2 years. This was an especially striking statistic if it is remembered that approximately 84% of the children had been in foster home care for at least 4 years. Approximately the same proportion of children, i.e., 16% had been carried by the same social worker for between 1 and 2 years. Two-thirds of the children had been in their social worker's caseload less than a year, and it may be remembered from the first part of this chapter that approximately 32% of the cases had no social worker assigned at all. Although it is one of the primary tasks of the social worker to help to resolve some of the issues which led to the necessity of foster home care, it is obvious that this won't be accomplished with caseload statistics such as these. On the other hand, if the child's return to the biological parent is unlikely, it is equally as improbable that a child would be free for adoption when there is not enough consistent professional attention to the child and the issues impinging on this status.

It would seem to be a relatively simple task to designate the criteria for determining which children should be referred to a special adoption unit or one established to provide intensive services to a family in order to expedite the return of a child. The Department, however, has labored under the pressures of crises for so long that such practices almost appear as luxury instead of necessity.

The consequences of short staffing pattern can be seen in other ways as well. One of the questions asked dealt with the length of time that elapsed since the last time the social worker saw the foster child. It can be seen from Table 2.14 that a substantial number of the children have very little, if any, contact with the social worker assigned to his or her case. In 23.2% of the cases, the last time a social worker saw the child in care is not known at all. Most of these are probably uncovered cases and, therefore, have not been

TABLE 2.14   Period of Time Elapsed Since Direct Contact of Social Worker with Child in Foster Home Care

Elapsed Time	N	%
Less than 1 month	1,269	21.6
1 month	469	25.1
2 months	663	11.3
3 months	354	6.0
4 to 6 months	387	6.6
7 to 9 months	123	2.1
10 to 12 months	85	1.4
13 to 18 months	54	1.0
19 to 24 months	32	.6
More than 24 months	67	1.1
Don't know	1,359	23.2
Total	5,862	100.0%

seen for some undetermined but probably protracted period. About 70% of the children have been seen within a 6-month period.

This fact is not, in and of itself, bad. There are undoubtedly large numbers of children who simply would not need to be seen if all other factors were under control. Children are seen or not seen depending on how productive the social worker is, the caseload pressures, the seriousness of problems which the child is presenting and the aggressiveness of the foster parents in demanding attention. Of greatest concern, and least defensible, is the fact that there are no guidelines established by the Department to decide when a case is designated as "uncovered," "active," or "inactive." Although it is clear that some supervisors are very conscientious about this issue, these designations occur as a matter of pressures related to issues often extraneous to the child's case. The end result is that there are hundreds of children, by and large, indiscriminately, who are not attended to for long periods of time.

An uncovered case in the Department of Public Welfare is one which does not have a social worker assigned who is immediately responsible for services to the child, his family, and foster home. These children are "covered" for emergencies by a supervisor at the district level or as a last resort by the Child Welfare Supervisor responsible for an entire geographical area of the Commonwealth. There is, in other words, neither an active casework plan for the child nor regular visits to the child, family, or foster home by a Department social worker. The foster parent, through a process of elimination, is responsible for the total care of the child and for obtaining assistance from a supervisor in the event of an emergency. There were, in November, 1971, approximately 1,690 uncovered cases in the Division of Family and Children's Services. Given that the Department had not been able to hire staff, even to replace many who resign or retire, that figure was substantially higher by the time of the original publication of this report. When it was released, early in 1973, the Governor "unfroze" over 300 public welfare positions. Once the effect of the Commission's investigation had passed, however, the earlier situation maintained.

A sensitive, and very important question must be raised with respect to this problem. Namely, what are the effects of leaving a case uncovered? More specifically, are there any differences in a child's chances for earlier restoration to his family or adoption if his case is covered or uncovered? Table 2.15 presents the data pertaining to length of time in care.

Many supervisors in the Department periodically judge which cases are in need of service and which seem to be more custodial in nature. This process is not at all universal to the supervisors and there are no established criteria by which the judgment is made. Table 2.15 shows that once a child is in foster home care for 2 years or more, he is significantly more likely to remain in care longer if his case is uncovered than if it is covered. Approximately 65% of the covered cases have been in foster home care for 2 years or longer compared with more than 78% of the uncovered cases. That fact, combined with the knowledge that a disproportionate number of the difficult cases are in the covered category clearly indicates that leaving a case uncovered may relegate the child to unnecessary long-term care. It is perfectly obvious that an uncovered case will not receive the services it needs if no one in a position to act can see them.

This conclusion can be tempered by recognizing that the proportion of covered cases in foster home care for less than 2 years is higher simply because there had to be a worker assigned at the point of intake. Attrition, decentralization, and other factors may not have left the case uncovered. Given that, the anticipated adoption of the child gives a more accurate picture of the consequences of a case being

TABLE 2.15 Comparison of Covered and Uncovered Cases by Length of Time Child Has Been in Foster Home Care*

Length of Time	Covered		Uncovered		Total	
	N	%**	N	%**	N	%**
6 months or less	415	84.5	76	15.5	491	100.0%
		(11.5)		(4.6)		(9.3)
7 to 11 months	302	78.4	83	21.6	385	100.0%
		(8.4)		(5.0)		(7.3)
12 to 23 months	549	73.4	199	26.6	748	100.0%
		(15.2)		(11.9)		(14.2)
24 to 59 months	936	64.3	519	35.7	1,455	100.0%
		(25.9)		(31.1)		(27.6)
60 to 119 months	980	64.1	548	35.9	1,528	100.0%
		(27.0)		(32.8)		(28.8)
10 years or more	432	64.0	243	36.0	675	100.0%
		(12.0)		(14.6)		(12.8)
Total	3,614	68.4	1,668	31.6	5,282	100.0%
		(100.0%)		(100.0%)		(100.0%)

$x^2 = 115.72$ df=5   p=<.001

*Cases in the care of private agencies were not considered in this table.
**Figures in parentheses refer to column percentages.

covered or uncovered. Table 2.16 presents the data for children for whom the social workers indicated that adoption has been considered at some time.

It can be seen from Table 2.16 that although uncovered cases represent about 32% of the Department's foster home care statistics, the proportion of children for whom adoption is anticipated is much lower than in covered cases. Of all the children in the covered caseloads, almost 1/4 of them can expect to be adopted at some future time, whereas less than 20% of their counterparts will probably be adopted. In line with that observation, it can be seen that the social workers do not know about the possibilities for adoption in 24.2% of the covered cases. Yet that figure jumps to 34.6% when the cases are uncovered.

Keeping in mind that all of the children represented in Table 2.16 have had adoption considered for them at some point, it is clear that there is a relationship between a case being covered and the probability of adoption actually occurring. The indications of negative consequences for uncovered cases seem to be rather clear.

One of the most obvious and potentially effective methods of resolving the problem of uncovered caseloads is to vest greater authority and responsibility in the foster parent. Since it is the foster parent who spends most of the time with the child and must contend with the various problems the child presents, it would make sense to allow foster parents to decide about the health and educational services which a child may need, just as they do for their own children. They could make these decisions in accordance with a set of clear but broad guidelines established by the Department. A small unit of professional personnel could then oversee and monitor foster parent functions. The foster parents would then be responsible for assuring that concrete services are provided to the child where necessary. This would, in turn, free the social workers from such activities as arranging for medical exams. The staff could be

TABLE 2.16 Comparison of Covered and Uncovered Cases by Whether or Not Adoption Is Anticipated*

Adoption Anticipated	Covered		Uncovered		Total	
	N	%	N	%	N	%
Yes, worker specified date by which adoption will occur	126	76.8 (3.5)	38	23.2 (2.3)	164	100.0%
Yes, but no date specified	637	71.7 (17.6)	251	28.3 (14.9)	888	100.0%
Yes, but worker has not referred the child	110	76.4 (3.0)	34	23.6 (2.0)	144	100.0%
No	1,870	70.6 (51.7)	778	29.4 (46.2)	2,648	100.0%

							100.0%
Don't know	876	60.1 (24.2)	582	39.9 (34.6)	1,458		100.0%
Total	3,619	68.3 (100.0%)	1,683	31.7 (100.0%)	5,302		

X²=68.56   df=4   p=<.001

*Cases in the care of private agencies were not considered in this table. Cases where consideration for adoption is not an applicable plan are not included in the data.
**Figures in parentheses refer to column percentages.

deployed in such a way as to focus on services which will lead to a permanent home for the child. The social workers, given an effective general monitoring system, would also be able to address special problems knowing that the foster parent is attending to cases which do not require special input.

In order to do this, the Department would have to make considerable change in its policies regarding foster parents. They would need to be trained and paid more for their added responsibility. Nonetheless, the associated cost would undoubtedly be less in the long run since the Department, in essence, would be establishing a mechanism for the differential use of personnel.

Related to this issue is the fact that the Department would have to establish mechanisms to give foster parents access to professionals in their communities, e.g., physicians, speech therapists, psychologists, etc, for their foster children to the same extent they have for their biological children. At present, the Medicaid system, (at least in Massachusetts) creates an inherent discriminatory process which complicates the difficulties which the foster parents already have in obtaining services. This is the case in many other states as well, i.e., service vendors wait very long periods of time to be paid for their services, if they are paid at all. When and if they are paid, the fee is often less than they would have received for a private patient.

It is probably true that the foster parents, under the provisions of the current system, actually assure that children in their care get, at least, the basic services which they require. More pertinent to the issue is that under the current system some of the foster parents appear to be divided into two extremes. At one end, there are those people who have volunteered their homes and families to provide care to the foster child as a matter of social conscience and personal commitment. At the other end, there are a few who view their role as a foster parent as one which is essentially an income-producing role in their family, albeit the income is small. There are too many cases on record where foster parents have been exceptionally lax in exercising their responsibilities. There is also considerable evidence where a small number have been outright abusive. It is no doubt true that these represent a small minority of the foster parents; however, there would be little disagreement that even a minute proportion of instances such as these are intolerable, given the minimal supervision.

The social workers were asked to rate the foster homes in which the children were placed. Their responses to that inquiry show that 39.3% of the homes were judged to be excellent, 35.8% were judged as good, 9.8% were rated as fair, and 2.8% were considered to be poor. Of much greater concern was the fact that in 12.4% of the cases the social workers were unable to rate the home because they were not familiar with it. Assuming that the social workers' familiarity allowed him to rate a foster home as poor in the first place, one might feel that some protection for a child existed. Where there has been no contact upon which to base a rating, then one must be concerned about the possible consequences for the foster child. That child is at substantial risk for being neglected by the Commonwealth.

The implications of this issue can be seen in even broader context if one thinks of the caseworker as one who can intervene appropriately to prevent crises which might necessitate the removal of the child from the foster home for reasons other than appropriate return to biological parents. One finds, however, when reviewing the data from this study, that approximately 25% of the children in foster home care have been moved from one foster home to another at least three times. The following distribution was obtained when the staff were asked about the total number of foster home placements since the child had been taken into care. It should be noted that this referred specifically to the child's entry into care this time as opposed to previous occasions when he may have been taken into care, returned to his biological parents, and taken into care again. The following obtained with regard to this issue: one placement, 50.4%; two placements, 24.9%; three placements, 11.5%; four to six placements, 9.5%; seven or more placements, 3.7%.

It can be seen from the above that movement from one foster home to another is a relatively frequent occurence although, frankly, not as great as was expected. Since our population of children is one which has experienced the traumatic removal from biological families, then one must assume that consequent removals from surrogate families only exacerbate the trauma. This may, indeed, reinforce the likelihood of psychological disorders occurring later in the child's life.

This problem seems to be related to staffing issues in that there are insufficient personnel to supervise and monitor the foster homes. This responsibility is distributed among large numbers of the Division's personnel and the system could be handled more efficiently and effectively if there were a specialized unit to take on such responsibilities.

Reviewing the data from just the last foster home move, it is noted that almost 30% of the children have been moved for reasons which are unknown to the social workers who completed the research instrument on the child. Over 26% of the children have been moved as a result of a direct request of the foster parent, usually because the child has been presenting a behavior problem. Slightly over 14% of the children were moved as a result of a general, unspecified agency decision and about 13% because the foster home was closed. The remaining approximately 17% were moved for such reasons as the child's request, court decision, biological parent took the child back and then returned him to foster home care again, and others.

Table 2.17 presents the data which were obtained

when the reasons for removal from the last two foster homes were compared. It can be seen that 2,442 children have been moved at least twice.

Indications of a number of problems appear in Table 2.17. These are especially related to the shortage of trained staff and their inability to intervene in situations which seem to be a risk. It can be seen, for instance, that of the 25.4% of the children who have been removed from a foster home due to their behavior problems, almost 1/3 had been removed previously for the same purpose. Similarly, of the 13.5% of the children removed for return to their biological parent, over 20% had been removed from the last foster home for the same reason. One can imagine the turmoil which a child experiences when moved back and forth from his biological home to foster home care.

These circumstances exist partly because the Department cannot deploy its staff so that they are available to intervene in situations which seem to be problematic. When the staff of the Department are so tied up trying to cover emergencies, they obviously cannot be available for prevention, regardless of how obvious the impending problem. Once again the "penny-wise, pound-foolish" policies often end up costing incalculably in human terms.

School Experience

Seventy-three percent of the children in foster home care actively attend school. Approximately 22% are preschool age and the remaining youths have either graduated or dropped out, with the exception of 20 children who stay at home as a result of illness. Almost 80% of those children who attend school do so in regular public day systems while about 7% attend special public day schools and an equal number attend private day schools. Almost 22% of the children are reported to be experiencing school problems of one type or another.

TABLE 2.17 Comparison of Reasons for Removal from Last Two Foster Homes

Reason for Removal	Same Reason Both Times		Different Reason Each Time		Total	
	N	%	N	%	N	%
Return to biological parent	72	16.0	258	13.0	330	13.5
Foster parent requested removal due to child's behavior problem	199	44.2	422	21.1	621	25.4
Foster parent requested removal due to problems with other children	10	2.2	106	5.3	116	4.8
Agency decision, home not good for child	39	8.7	376	18.9	415	17.0
Child ran away	22	4.9	95	4.8	117	4.8
Court decision	0	0.0	13	0.7	13	0.5

Change within foster home, e.g., death in family	38	8.4	269	13.5	307	12.6
Other	70	15.6	453	22.7	523	21.4
Total	450	100.0%	1,992	100.0%	2,442	100.0%

$x^2 = 128.57$ df=7   p=<.001

NOTES

1. Shirley Jenkins and Mignon Sauber, *Paths to Child Placement* (New York: The Community Council of Greater New York, 1966), pp. 62–66.

2. This category includes current pregnancy which may have necessitated confinement.

3. Percentages in parentheses refer to proportions of children placed for that reason in New York City.

Chapter 3

THE HANDICAPPED CHILD IN FOSTER HOME CARE—I

INTRODUCTION

The idea of utilizing foster homes as an alternative to institutionalization for developmentally disabled children is certainly not new. There are obviously very serious needs for "alternatives to warehousing" of such children and a number of reports have cited foster home care as one of the most viable.[1]

Placing the handicapped child in a foster home is not without its very serious problems, however. In Massachusetts, the Department of Public Welfare does not explicitly identify those foster homes which are designated for a disabled child. This is in spite of the fact that there is some indication that such designation has value.[2]

The Massachusetts Governor's Commission on Adoption and Foster Care discovered that approximately 40% of the children in foster home care are disabled in some way.[3]

This figure is much higher than that which would be found in a normal population. If it were not, as will be seen, for the fact that the children are so often seriously neglected, the concept of the foster home as a place for such children would have great credence.

Before looking at the research findings, however, one should be aware of the theoretical value of such programs for the handicapped child whose family is either unwilling or unable to care for him.

Garrett[4] has noted that "most appropriately foster family service often results in more progress and less misery for the mentally retarded child. It may also save money, but how much can desirably be saved is questionable. One study has indicated that foster family placement of 24 children saved a state $200,000 in 1 year.[5] The question, however, is whether the program *should* have saved that much money. Were the foster families not sufficiently reimbursed or the children's special needs not met?"

The President's Committee on Mental Retardation[6] noted that there are two extremely important concepts to be considered when working with the mentally retarded child. These concepts are equally important for children handicapped in other ways. They have been called *normalization* and *human management.*[7]

Garrett stated that normalization "refers to designing programs for mentally retarded children so that they will:

1. "Enable the child to behave in a way that will lead others to perceive him as not too different from other children—or at least as little different as possible.
2. "Help others see the child's strengths and similarities to other children so that his differences from others will be minimized.
3. "Help people in general gain a broader perspective of what is normal and acceptable in child development."

She goes on to note that there are four principles which derive from the normalization concept and apply to foster family care. They are (1) integration—creating and promoting opportunities for the child to interact in the community, (2) dispersal—only placing as many disabled children in a particular community as can be effectively absorbed into community life, (3) specialization—developing a team of professionals who have expertise in developmental disabilities, and (4) continuity—ensuring the involvement of the child's natural family so long as this is in his best interests.

The human management concept applies equally to the child and his/her parents. Garrett notes that it has three main requirements:

1.   "That the child's parents be regarded by the helping staff as normal persons under unusual stress and not be 'denormalized' by being regarded as different from other parents.

2.   "That with rare exceptions the foster family be used only to supplement and not supplant the role of the child's own family. Next in importance to maintenance of life for the child is maintenance of his place within his family.

3.   "That decisions regarding structure, policy, and individual problems be measured by whether they best meet the individual needs of the parents and child, not by whether they promote medical, institutional, or program 'efficiency'."

The basic proposition of this report is that these concepts are currently not utilized in foster home care by either the public or private agencies for developmentally disabled children, at least not in Massachusetts. In large part, this is because the issues have never been collected and presented in such a way as to create the opportunity to implement the concepts.

IDENTIFYING INFORMATION

As noted above, almost 40% of the children placed in foster home care in Massachusetts, in 1971, were handicapped
in some way other than the fact of their foster child status.
At the time of this writing (1975), no major changes have
as yet been affected in the Commonwealth, thus there is no
reason to believe that the situation has undergone any substantial change.

Table 3.1 presents the data pertaining to the types of
disabilities discovered.

Of the entire population, only 41 children were found
to be placed in foster homes independent of the Massachusetts Department of Public Welfare. Even though it was
shown previously that over 11% of all foster children in the
Commonwealth are placed in homes supervised by private
agencies, it was discovered that almost 80% of those placements are paid for under contract with the Department.
Consequently, foster home care for the handicapped child
is almost entirely a public function. Of the 41 children in
private agency foster homes who are not financially supported by the state, 16 are fully supported by their parents
or guardians. The majority of the remainder receive partial
support either from their parents or third party payers,
such as Social Security or Veteran's Benefits.

The average age of a handicapped child in foster home
care is 9 years old. About 3% of the children (57) are less
than 1 year old, and approximately 23% (403) are between
1 and 6. About 1/3 of the children (569) are between 6 and
10 years old, while almost 27% (462) are between 11 and
15. Approximately 13% (230) are 16 years old or older.
The age distribution of the handicapped children is not
substantially different from that of non-handicapped children except for those under 1 year old. Approximately 7%
of the total population of children in foster home care are
less than 1 year old. Yet only about 3% of the handicapped

TABLE 3.1[8] Type and Frequency of Disabilities Found in Children in Foster Home Care

Type of Disability	N	%
Arm/hand use	90	2.4
Leg/foot use	228	6.0
Vision	332	8.7
Hearing	146	3.8
Speech	297	7.8
Toilet functions	115	3.0
Convulsive	90	2.4
Physical disfigurement	76	2.0
Other medical	485	12.7
Intellectual	705	18.5
Behavior/emotional	1,250	32.7
Total	3,814*	100.0%

*The total of 3,814 refers to the frequency of disabilities, not the number of children. Approximately 15% of the children have multiple disabilities.

children, as mentioned, are that young. Assuming that the child's handicap is at least a contributing factor in his placement, then this finding is consistent with the fact that many handicapping conditions are not identifiable until a child is beyond infancy.

As can be seen from Table 3.2, a handicapped male is more likely to be placed in a foster home than a handicapped female. Of the children for whom data were available, over 56% were males. This is compared to the fact that there is a relatively even split between the sexes among the nonhandicapped general foster child population. There is no immediately obvious reason for this discrepancy other than that boys may be more difficult to manage and, therefore, less likely to be maintained in their own homes.

The racial/ethnic distribution of handicapped children in foster home care can be seen in Table 3.3. When the racial identifications of the children are compared as shown in Table 3.4, however, it can be seen that black children with handicaps are less apt to be found in foster home care than their non-black counterparts. This is likely related to the difficulties encountered in obtaining services when the prospective recipients of those services are both black and poor. It is suspected that further analysis of these data would indicate that the differences in frequency of handicapping conditions are most likely to be found in the areas of emotional/behavioral problems. A follow-up study using data from the Governor's Commission on Foster Home Care Study was recently conducted. It was discovered that black children are significantly less likely to come into foster home care for the reason of mental illness of the parent than were white children.[9] This was primarily attributed to the lack of mental health services in the black communities. One must, after all, have access to mental health services to even be categorized as being officially unable to cope with one's children.

TABLE 3.2 Comparison of Sex of Handicapped and Non-Handicapped Children in Foster Home Care*

Sex	Handicapped N	%	Not Handicapped N	%	Total N	%
Male	957	31.2 (56.3)	2,111	68.8 (51.5)	3,068	100.0% (52.9)
Female	743	27.2 (43.7)	1,988	72.8 (48.5)	2,731	100.0% (47.1)
Total	1,700	(100.0%)	4,099	(100.0%)	5,799	(100.0%)

*Percentages in parentheses refer to columns.

$x^2 = 11.08$ df=1   p=<.001

79

TABLE 3.3 Racial/Ethnic Identification of Handicapped Children in Foster Home Care

Race/Ethnic I.D.	N	%
White	1,379	80.1
Black	211	12.3
Interracial B/W	52	3.0
Interracial other	39	2.3
Spanish-speaking	24	1.4
American Indian	6	.3
Other	5	.3
Don't know	5	.3
Total	1,721	100.0%

As can be seen in Table 3.5, the largest proportion of the handicapped children in foster home care are Catholics, with Protestants running second.

With respect to the legal status of handicapped children in foster home care, it can be seen from Table 3.6 that 56% of the children have been placed in a foster home on a voluntary basis. If one combines the voluntary and temporary categories in Table 3.6, it is noted that over 65% of the children are in foster homes either on a voluntary or temporary basis. The implication, therefore, is that almost two-thirds of the children in foster home care should theoretically be discharged to their own families at some not too

TABLE 3.4 Comparison of Race of Handicapped Children in Foster Home Care*

	White		Black		Other		Total	
Condition of Child	N	%	N	%	N	%	N	%
Handicapped	1,379	80.4 (30.4)	263	15.3 (25.0)	74	4.3 (29.5)	1,716	100.0% (29.4)
Not Handi-capped	3,158	76.6 (69.6)	789	19.1 (75.0)	177	4.3 (70.5)	4,124	100.0% (70.6)
Total	4,537	(100.0%)	1,052	(100.0%)	251	100.0%	5,840	(100.0%)

*Children designated as interracial: black and white, were combined with those designated as black.

**Percentages in parentheses refer to columns.

$x^2=12$ df=2   p=<.01

TABLE 3.5   Religion of Handicapped Children in Foster Home Care

Religion	N	%
Catholic	1,012	58.7
Protestant	612	35.6
Jewish	16	.9
Other	15	.9
None	27	1.6
Don't know	39	2.3
Total	1,721	100.0%

distant future time. As will be noted in later sections, how-ever, this does not seem to coincide with the reality of the length of time which a child is actually in care.

THE PLACEMENT

As can be seen from Table 3.7, the most frequent reason given for placement of a handicapped child in foster home care is mental illness of a parent. Neglect, abuse, or inadequate home account for approximately 15% of the placements, with physical illness of a parent accounting for slightly less than 10%. These reasons are consistent with the data for all foster children, handicapped and nonhandicapped. The reasons of mental illness of parent, neglect or abuse or inadequate home, physical illness of parent, and

TABLE 3.6 Legal Status of Handicapped Children in Foster Home Care

Legal Status	N	%
Voluntary (private)	157	9.1
Voluntary (public)	808	46.9
Child of incarcerated mother	22	1.3
Temporary custody probate court	56	3.3
Permanent custody probate court	42	2.4
Permanent custody probate court with adoption release	21	1.2
Temporary custody district court	100	5.8
Permanent custody district court	349	20.3
Permanent custody district court with adoption release	26	1.5
Hearing pending	21	1.2
Appeal pending	17	1.0
Other	95	5.5
Unknown	7	.5
Total	1,721	100.0%

TABLE 3.7 Reason for Placement of Handicapped Child in Foster Home Care*

Reason	N	%
Mental illness of parent	571	27.1
Neglect, abuse, or inadequate home	327	15.5
Physical illness of parent	199	9.4
Divorce or desertion	185	8.8
Abandonment	178	8.3
Mother deciding whether to keep baby or place for adoption	161	7.5
Foster placement recommended as part of treatment plan for child's emotional disturbance	125	5.8
Death of parent	86	4.0
Parent(s) in jail	82	3.8
Mother hospitalized or bedridden	58	2.7
Referral from juvenile court after committing offense	47	2.2
Child ran away from home	44	2.1
Drug addiction/alcoholism of parents	40	1.9
Awaiting adoption (child of unmarried mother)	20	.9
Total	2,138	100.0%

mother deciding whether to keep baby or place for adoption are slightly higher for the handicapped children than for their nonhandicapped counterparts.

It is likely that foster home care placements could probably be substantially reduced if viable options, such as homemaker services, were available to social workers and the families. Even beyond this, one must raise the question of the adequacy of medical care available to poor families. It is clear that such care is not readily available.

More than 2/3 of the children were living with one or both parents just prior to their placement in foster home care. Less than 8% of the children were institutionalized prior to that time. Slightly over 20% of the referrals are directly from the parent of the child to the Department of Public Welfare without any intermediary. There are 14% of the referrals from the court, and an additional 14% from some institution such as a school or hospital. About 40% of the referrals originated in a private social agency.

Once a handicapped child has been referred and placed, the average length of time which he will remain in a foster home is almost 6 years, almost 1 year longer than all foster children spend. If all of the handicapped children were removed from that original population, then a substantial discrepancy would exist between the predicted length of placement of a handicapped child and a nonhandicapped child. By the very fact that the child is handicapped, given current conditions, he is much less likely to be either returned to his biological family or placed for adoption.

---

*There were 1,721 handicapped children in this study. Some of these children were placed for more than one reason and the records do not indicate which was primary. The data in Table 3-7, therefore, refer to reasons rather than children.

Eight percent of the children had been previously placed in foster home care with another agency, and an additional 48% of the children had been previously placed in foster home care with the current agency. This figure represents a remarkable difference between handicapped and nonhandicapped children. The original Governor's Commission study on the total foster children population found that only about 16% of the children had previously been placed in foster home care. Of those children, almost 3/4 had been placed only one time before. In comparison, as has been presented above, 56% of the handicapped children have been placed previously. Forty-seven percent of those children have been placed between two and four times.

Table 3.8 represents some of the data identifying the multiplicity of foster home placements of handicapped children as a major problem. The vast majority of these multiple placements indicate prior foster home failures, and the need to rectify the conditions which cause the chronic instability.

At the time of initial entry into foster home care, almost 40% of the children (688) were stated to be entering care for some specified length of time. However, 82% of the children (1,409) have never been returned to their biological parents even for a trial period.

Regarding parent interest in the child in foster home care, it can be seen in Table 3.6 that only about 25% of the handicapped foster children have been placed with the legal status of permanent custody with or without adoption release from either the probate or district courts. The subsequent assumption is that the 75% of foster children who are placed with other legal statuses are in foster homes temporarily until they can be reunited with their biological families. Assuming that the frequency of parent contact with the child is a relatively reliable index of parent interest, then there would appear to be a major discrepancy

TABLE 3.8 Total Number of Foster Home Placements of Handicapped Children		
Total Number of Placements*	N	%
1	758	44.1
2	445	25.9
3	234	13.6
4	129	7.5
5	52	3.0
6	30	1.7
7	21	1.2
8	13	.8
9 or more	16	.9
Don't know	23	1.3
	1,721	100.0%

*Includes current placement.

between the legal status of the child and the frequency of parent contact. Specifically, Table 3.9 shows that less than 35% of the children (598) have seen their parents at least one time in a given 6 month period. Less than 22% of the children (372) have seen one of their parents or guardians once within a 2 month period. These data are consistent with those reported in the original Governor's Commission report on all children in foster care. Therefore, there does not appear to be any greater a problem in considering this issue when focusing on foster children who are handicapped than when focusing on foster children in general. The fact of the matter remains, however, that most of these children appear to have been abandoned by their biological families, and the likelihood of their being returned is extremely doubtful. The consequence is that plans must be made for each of these children with the recognition that they will be in long term care. This fact is further supported by the social worker's predictions that only slightly more than 22% of the children (385) have any chance at all of ultimately being legally adopted.

TABLE 3.9 Frequency of Parent Contact of Handicapped Children in Foster Home Care

Frequency of Parent Contact (Approximate)	N	%
Once a week or more	61	3.5
Twice a month	99	5.8
Once a month	140	8.1
Once every 2 months	72	4.2
Once every 3 months	87	5.1
Once in 6 months	139	8.1
Never during 6 month period in question	954	55.4
Don't know	169	9.8
Total	1,721	100.0%

SERVICES TO THE HANDICAPPED CHILDREN

As part of this study, the social workers carrying primary case responsibility—or supervisors of cases which were uncovered—were asked to indicate the frequency with which the children's disabilities had been formally evaluated by qualified professionals. Table 3.10 presents the data comparing the frequency of disability with the frequency of evaluations.

The lack of evaluation of a foster child's disability was one of the most serious problems uncovered in the Governor's Commission report regarding the care received by a child who was under the supervision of the Massachusetts Department of Public Welfare. It can be seen from Table 3.10, for instance, that significant proportions of children, who were identified as being disabled, have not had any process begun to treat the handicap. Fifteen percent of the children who had seizures had not been seen by a physician. Almost 25% of the children who presented indications of being mentally retarded had never been seen by a neuropsychologist, neurologist, or even psychometrist. Almost 30% of the children with behavioral or emotional problems have never been seen by a mental health professional. Thirty-two percent of the children with speech difficulty have never been seen by a speech pathologist. Half of the children with toilet function disorders have never been seen for an assessment of that problem.

The issues related to handicapping conditions present in a foster child were taken beyond the question of evaluation by the Governor's Commission. Social workers were asked to indicate the dates that a recommended treatment program was implemented for a foster child whose disability had been evaluated by an appropriate professional. As can be seen from Table 3.11, in many cases, either the treatment program had not been implemented or the social worker had no assurance that it had been. Even assuming

**TABLE 3.10 Type and Frequency of Disabilities and
Frequency of Professional Evaluation of Those
Disabilities in Children in Foster Home Care**

Type of Disability	Evaluated N	Evaluated %	Not Evaluated N	Not Evaluated %	Total N	Total %
Arm/hand use	81	90.0	9	10.0	90	100.0
Leg/foot use	198	86.8	30	13.2	228	100.0
Vision	302	91.0	30	9.0	332	100.0
Hearing	133	91.1	13	8.9	146	100.0
Speech	202	68.0	95	32.0	297	100.0

Toilet functions	57	49.6	58	50.4	115	100.0
Convulsive	78	86.7	12	13.3	90	100.0
Physical disfigurement	60	78.9	16	21.1	76	100.0
Other medical	388	80.0	97	20.0	485	100.0
Intellectual	533	75.6	172	24.4	705	100.0
Behavior/emotional	879	70.3	371	29.7	1,250	100.0
Total	2,911*	76.3%	903*	23.7%	3,814*	100.0%

*Totals refer to disabilities, not children.

TABLE 3.11 Whether or Not Recommended Treatment Program Was Implemented for Foster Child's Disability*

Type of Disability	Treatment Program Recommended and Implemented		Treatment Program Recommended but Not Implemented		Total	
	N	%	N	%	N	%
Arm/hand use	27	64.3 (1.9)	15	35.7 (3.0)	42	100.0
Leg/foot use	34	23.4 (2.4)	111	76.6 (22.4)	145	100.0
Vision	194	82.9 (13.9)	40	17.1 (8.1)	234	100.0
Hearing	65	100.0 (4.7)	0	0.0 (0.0)	65	100.0
Speech	111	76.0 (8.0)	35	24.0 (7.1)	146	100.0
Toilet function	23	62.2 (1.6)	14	37.8 (2.8)	37	100.0
Convulsive	55	100.0 (3.9)	0	0.0 (0.0)	55	100.0

	Count	% (%)	Count	% (%)	Count	%
Physical disfigurement	40	100.0 (2.9)	0	0.0 (0.0)	40	100.0
Other medical	232	89.9 (16.6)	26	10.1 (5.2)	258	100.0
Intellectual	195	83.0 (14.0)	40	17.0 (8.1)	235	100.0
Behavior/emotional	418	66.0 (30.1)	215	34.0 (43.3)	633	100.0
Total	1,394**	73.8% (100.0%)	496**	26.2% (100.0%)	1,890**	100.0%

*Figures in parenthesis refer to percentages by column.
**Figures represent frequency of disabilities, not children.

93

that the latter is more likely than the former, these data indicate a serious problem.

It can be seen from Table 3.11 that more than a quarter of the children evaluated and recommended for treatment had either not yet had that treatment program implemented or, more accurately, the social worker assigned to the child's case did not know if the recommended treatment program had been implemented. In most cases follow-up showed that it, in fact, had not.

In general, the reasons treatment programs had not been implemented were mostly unknown. In answer to the question, "If a recommended treatment has not yet been implemented, why not?", the social worker's responses presented the following distribution: 1) no available funds, 7.9%; 2) no available services, child is on waiting list, 19.3%; 3) no available services where child is living, 10.9%; 4) foster parent reluctant about treatment, 4.2%; 5) natural parent reluctant about treatment, 2.3%; 6) child reluctant about treatment, 10.6%, 7) short staff, heavy caseload, 17.0%; and 8) other, 27.9%.

FOLLOW-UP DATA

This study obtained follow-up data on 1,421 children who were previously identified as handicapped. Two had died since November, 1971, according to the data of the Governor's Commission study. Three others had died prior to this study, but they are not included in the 1,721 children on whom data are available. Almost 3/4 of the children were still in the same foster home in January, 1973, as they were in November, 1971. Over 2/3 of the children have been in foster home care more than 2 years, and over 1/3 of those have been in care for more than 5 years.

Approximately 2/3 of the children (252) were reported to have emotional problems. It was found that of these children a substantially higher percentage have been moved from one foster home to another. Many more have problems which are moderate to severe when compared to the children reported to be experiencing emotional difficulties but who remain in their original foster home. It is more likely that the child's emotional disturbance brought about the change of foster home than that the foster home change caused the child's problems. One might expect, however, that the instability of the placement exacerbates the child's disorder.

It is clear that the children who are designated as having emotional problems, particularly severe emotional problems, are the children who switch homes most often. Given that an "emotional problem" is a rather nebulous category, one cannot help but raise the question about whether or not this is a traditional rationale that foster parents use when requesting that a child be moved from their home. Assuming, however, that an emotional disorder actually exists and is the cause of a child's inability to be maintained in the foster home, it is clear from data presented previously that services are either unavailable or not utilized to reduce the problems.

It can be seen from Table 3.12 that less than half of the disabilities fall in the moderate to severe category. The exception to this is in the area of convulsive disorders where 2/3 of the children have been classified as moderate or severe. Reported as taking medications for seizures were 72 children, and of those, 50 were classified as moderate or severe, 6 were reported as experiencing mild seizures, and 8 children present uncertain/unknown seizure activity though they are taking medication. Another 8 children were reported as taking seizure medication but were not indicated as having a convulsive disorder.

A high proportion of children in the moderate or severe category have learning problems. Slightly more than 1/2 of all the children who are reported as handicapped

TABLE 3.12 Frequency and Severity of Handicaps in Children in Foster Home Care

Type of Disability	N*		%**	
Arm/hand use	101	(29)***	5.8	(1.6)
Leg/foot use	181	(55)	10.4	(3.0)
Vision	528	(72)	30.5	(4.1)
Hearing	151	(40)	8.7	(2.2)
Speech	425	(148)	24.6	(8.5)
Toilet training	394	(183)	22.8	(10.5)
Convulsive disorder	110	(74)	6.3	(4.2)
Physical disfigurement	160	(21)	9.2	(1.1)
Other medical (limiting activities)	179	(63)	10.3	(3.6)
Other medical	286	(88)	16.5	(5.0)
Emotional	841	(373)	48.6	(21.5)
Behavior control	717	(251)	41.5	(14.5)
Slow learner	893	(443)	51.7	(25.6)
Limited in routine	497	(207)	28.7	(11.9)

*Refers to frequency of handicaps, not children.
**Base figure for percentages is 1,721 children, rather than 5,463 specific handicaps.
***Numbers in parentheses refer to children whose problems have been designated as moderate or severe.

were classified as "slow learners," and approximately 1/4 of the children were classified as moderate or severe. The validity of that classification is supported by the fact that only about 7% of the children attend regular school classes.

Looking further at school attendance, it was found that 47.9% of the children classified as being emotionally disturbed or experiencing behavior problems were in regular school classes. This compares with 7.9% of those children designated as mentally retarded and 22.5% of the children with cerebral palsy. While it is clear that there is a movement to keep these children integrated with the total school population, a serious question must be raised as to whether large numbers of children with special problems are being deprived of the special services they need in order to succeed in their educational careers. The evidence would suggest that, given current policies and programs, those services were unavailable.

Considerable problems were identified regarding the point of view foster parents took of the foster child's disability. When the foster parents were asked about the existence of handicaps in their foster children, 240 (13.8%) replied that the child did *not* have a problem, in spite of the fact that the child had already been so identified. Interestingly, the foster parents still completed the questionnaire in each of the 240 cases and proceeded to describe the previously unacknowledged disability. It was found that the disparity was most frequent in the area of vision difficulties (58 children). This is probably to be expected since many people would consider the necessity of wearing corrective lenses to be "no problem" even though, technically, a problem of visual acuity exists. Only one of these children was categorized as having a moderate-severe problem.

In relative comparison to the total group, there was a higher percentage of children with hearing problems unacknowledged by foster parents than might be expected, i.e.,

13 children out of a total of 191. The same observation was made in the area of general medical problems which limit participation. Out of a total population of 242 children, 27 were said to have "no problem" by the foster parent.

On the other hand, it was noted that children designated as emotionally disturbed were seldom categorized as having "no problem" by the foster parents. In the total population, emotional problems were second only to learning problems in frequency. In the "no problem" group, however, emotional problems ranked seventh in frequency. It may be hypothesized that children with emotional and behavioral difficulties create so many problems for their foster parents that it is extremely difficult to pass off the situation as nonproblematic.

Perhaps most important in this disparity between the actual existence of a handicap and the assessment of a foster parent is the fact that, though the "no problem" children do indeed have some handicapping condition, these disabilities and the children themselves are not seen as problems by the foster parents or the children.

Table 3.13 presents the data relating to the type of professional active in a treatment program or in the general support of the children in foster home care. About half (871 out of 1,727) are specifically involved with one or more professionals.

As can be seen from Table 3.13, over 1/4 of the children see a social worker periodically, but only about 12% of the population have contact at least once every 2 weeks. Slightly over 20% visit a physician sporadically, while less than 4% do so at least every other week.

Although 16% of the children have difficulty with arm/hand or leg/foot use, only 3.6% periodically see a physical therapist and 1.5% do so frequently. Some of the other cases fare somewhat better. Slightly less than 25% of the children present some speech problem, and almost 8%

at least sporadically see a speech therapist. Most of these contacts are on a relatively frequent basis.

Almost half of the children were designated as having some emotional problem. It can be seen that about 11% are seeing guidance counselors, slightly more than 9% are seeing psychologists, about 7% see a psychiatrist, and over 25% see a social worker. We do not know, however, how many of the contacts with guidance counselors and social workers are actually for therapy. In any event, assuming that emotional problems cannot be treated on a sporadic basis, it can be seen that only about 1/4 of these contacts are with a frequency of at least every other week. That figure is liberal since it cannot be assumed that all of the social work and guidance contacts are psychotherapeutic in nature. It must also be taken into consideration that there are unduplicated counts and, therefore, a particular child can be seeing a social worker, a guidance counselor, and a psychiatrist all at the same time. The conclusion is that mental health services are among the most needed and least available for this group of children.

Table 3.13 indicated that, given frequent contact, social workers, guidance counselors, and speech therapists are the major service providers for disabled foster children. In spite of the staff shortages in the Department of Public Welfare, social workers remain the major service providers for foster children. The two other major professional groups are the guidance counselors and speech therapists, both of which are almost always employed through the public schools. It can be clearly seen then, that even though this population is identified as handicapped, they primarily receive services from professionals generally employed in the public sector and considered to be at the lower end of skilled professionals. It is a reasonable hypothesis that children who remain with their own families in their home communities receive services from more highly trained professionals on a more frequent basis.

TABLE 3.13 Type of Professional Active in the Treatment or Support of Disabled Children in Foster Home Care

Service Provider	No. of Children Active but Seen Infrequently		No. of Children Active and Seen at Least Every Other Week	
	N	%	N	%*
Social Worker	499	27.6	215	11.9
Physician	371	20.5	69	3.8
Guidance counselor	201	11.1	131	7.2
Psychologist	172	9.5	69	3.8
Speech therapist	140	7.7	115	6.4
Psychiatrist	133	7.3	60	3.3
Physical therapist	65	3.6	28	1.5
Special education teacher	65	3.6	57	3.1

Nurse	51	2.8	20	1.1
Minister	41	2.3	21	1.2
Occupational therapist	32	1.8	15	.8
Other, e.g., probation officer, professional foster parent, dentist, etc.	40	2.2	0	0
Total	1,810	100.0%	800	44.1%

*Percentage calculated on base of 1,810.

STAFF

Given the traditionally high attrition rate of the Department of Public Welfare, continuity of care has always been a difficult problem to contend with. Only about 19% of the handicapped foster children (330), for instance, had been in their social worker's caseload for a period of more than 2 years. Approximately the same number (307) had been carried by the same social worker for between 1 and 2 years. Of greatest concern is the fact that 25% of the cases at the time of the Governor's Commission study had no social worker assigned to them at all, i.e., they were designated as uncovered.

It is obviously very unlikely that the social worker can help to resolve some of the issues which led to the necessity of foster home care when cases are uncovered or caseloads are impossibly high. If return to the biological parent is unlikely, it is equally as improbable that a child will be freed for adoption when there is not enough consistency and professional attention to insure that someone on the staff is familiar with the child and the issues impinging on his status.

It was noted earlier that one of the major problems uncovered in this study is the multiple placement and rate of failure of foster home placements of handicapped children. It was also found that almost 20% of the children (212) have been moved for reasons which are unknown to the social workers who completed the original research instrument on the child. Over 27% of the children (299) have been moved as a result of a direct request of a foster parent, usually because the children present problems which are too difficult to contend with in the context of their foster home and the resources available to them. Almost 15% of the children (1630) have been moved from their last foster home due to an agency decision which was generally for relatively unspecified reasons. About 12% of the children (129) have been moved because the foster home was closed. The remaining children were moved for such reasons as the child's request, court decision, biological parent taking the child back and then returning him to a foster home again, and others.

As noted above, for whatever the reasons, these data are not significantly different from those gathered for the entire population of children in foster care in Massachusetts. The fact of the matter remains, however, that handicapped children must be considered to be children "at risk" and certainly need enough continuity of care to assure that their handicaps are dealt with adequately.

NOTES

1. See, for instance, Doris S. Fraser, *Perceived Dependence—Independence Derivations and Duplications of an Empirically Based Factor in Planning for Residents in Public Institutions for the Mentally Retarded in Massachusetts.* (Commonwealth of Massachusetts, Executive Office for Administration and Finance, Bureau of Developmental Disabilities, 1971.)

2. Richard A. Mamula, "The Use of Developmental Plans for Mentally Retarded Children in Foster Family Care," *Children* (March–April, 1971).

3. Alan R. Gruber, *Foster Home Care in Massachusetts: A Study of Foster Children—Their Biological and Foster Parents.* (Boston: Governor's Commission on Adoption and Foster Care, 1973), p. 33.

4. Beatrice L. Garrett, "Foster Family Services for Mentally Retarded Children," *Children,* (November–December, 1970).

5. Ruth Wade Cox and Mary Hamilton James, "Rescue from Limbo: Foster Home Placement for Hospitalized, Physically Disabled Children," *Child Welfare,* (January, 1970).

6. President's Committee on Mental Retardation, *MR '69: Toward Progress: The Story of a Decade.* Report of the PCMR. (Washington, D.C. 1969).

7. Gunnar Dybwad, "Action Implications, U.S.A." *Changing Patterns in Residential Services for the Retarded.* (Washington, D.C.: President's Committee on Mental Retardation, 1969).

Bengt Nirje, "The Normalization Principle and Its Human Management Implications." *Ibid.*

8. The research instrument used for this study utilized descriptive terms concerning functional problems rather than clinical/diagnostic labels. The dimensions were developed with the assistance of the staff of the Massachusetts Bureau of Developmental Disabilities. Dr. Doris Fraser and Carol Markowitz were especially helpful in this regard.

9. Jacquelyn L. Brown, et al., "Foster Home Care: Black Parents vs. White Parents' Reasons for Placement," Boston University School of Social Work Master Thesis, Unpublished, 1973.

Chapter 4

THE HANDICAPPED CHILD IN
FOSTER HOME CARE—II

INTRODUCTION

A sample of 100 children was selected from the population of handicapped foster children in order to determine the particulars regarding treatment of their disabilities and the problems foster parents encountered in obtaining such treatment. A weighting system was developed by the Project staff to determine the severity of a given disability. The weighting system accorded the highest scores to those children with the most severe disability. Additional weight was given if a child presented cerebral palsy, epilepsy or mental retardation.[1] The sample consists of the most severely disabled children in the population who were originally reported as having one of the three target conditions. As it turned out, however, a close survey of the medical records indicated that 10 of the children had neither cerebral palsy, epilepsy or mental retardation although their social workers or foster parents indicated that they did.

Four of the children in the sample had to be excluded due to the fact that adequate data were unavailable. As a result, this section deals with the experiences of the 96 most severely disabled children in foster home care in Massachusetts on the target date of the study, November 18, 1971.

METHODOLOGY

In order to obtain further information regarding treatment, facilities utilized, professional contacts and other data relating to the care of the disabled child, the foster parent(s) who had originally completed the disability questionnaire was telephoned. A series of questions were asked, such as: "Who is the primary service provider for this child?" "How often does the child see this person?" "Is the child taking medication?" "How much?" "How often?" "What types of extra care are needed in the foster home?" "Have there been any problems in obtaining treatment or other services for the child?" "What kinds of problems?" In addition, names and addresses of professionals who deal with the child for various reasons were obtained. The child's current social worker was also identified.

The second step in obtaining specific data regarding services for these children was to contact the Division of Family and Children's Service (DFCS) District Office which was responsible for the care of the child. The DFCS social worker was then contacted and asked a series of similar questions to those asked of the foster parent. A series of questions related to the child's legal status, the identification of the child's biological parents, and others were also asked.

Concurrent with the above, permission to release medical information on each of the children was obtained from either the Department or the biological parent(s) of the child if they were available. These forms were then forwarded to physicians, hospitals, clinics, and other providers of professional services identified earlier. The information requested pertained to services provided, specific diagnoses, problems in providing services, and other relevant facts. Summaries from the records of each child were requested. Responses were received from 47 independent professionals and 20 hospitals, clinics, and other institutions. In addition, 204 social workers were contacted. More than 25% of the children had information provided by all four sources: foster parents, social workers, independent professionals, and community institutions.

It should be noted that all of these children were in the care of the Massachusetts Department of Public Welfare, Division of Family and Children's Services, at the time of this study. This fact emphasizes that the children with the most serious difficulties are invariably in the care of the public, rather than the private, sector. Only 3% of the handicapped children in this study were in the care of private organizations. It was this fact that prohibited the comparison of the experiences of children in public and private agencies. Many studies have indicated that although private agencies present considerably more positive statistics on their provision of child welfare services, they have often failed to account for the fact that the public agencies cannot be as selective in their intake policies. The consequence is that the populations are not comparable.

It must be emphasized, nonetheless, that of the 96 children in the sample, 18 were reported as uncovered, i.e., there was no social worker assigned to the case. The length of time that the child had been with a social worker ranged from 2 months to 2 1/2 years. There were 8 children uncovered for less than 1 year and the remaining 10 for periods of 1 year or more. Twenty-nine more cases were identified as having been uncovered before being chosen for this phase of the study. Thus, almost 1/2 the sample had been uncovered in the 6 months prior to selection for the Project, a situation particularly unconscionable in light of the fact that these children were identified as the most severely disabled in foster home care. These facts obviously emphasize the need for funding of services to these children in a system which is subject to accountability.

IDENTIFYING DATA

The children in this sample were found to be younger than those in the total foster home care population. Table 4.1 shows that the average age of the severely developmentally disabled child is 7.8 years compared to 10.5 years in the population.

The children in this sample have been in foster home care for shorter periods of time than those children in the total foster home care population. The average child in a foster home can be expected to have been there for slightly over 5 years. In comparison, the child with a severe developmental disability can be expected to have been in the foster home for just less than 4-1/2 years. There are three considerations to explain the difference: 1) the developmentally disabled child is generally younger than his non-disabled counterparts, 2) life expectancies are shorter as a consequence of the disease, and 3) as the child ages, problems in child management and care increase, thereby making institutionalization necessary.

Regarding the distribution by sex, males significantly outnumbered females as approximately 57% of the children are male.

THE HANDICAPS AND CARE

Table 4.2 shows the diagnoses listed for the children in the sample. It can be seen that the total number is substantially greater than 96. The reason is that many children present multiple problems.

TABLE 4.1 Comparison of Ages of Severely Developmentally Disabled Children and the Total Population of Children in Foster Home Care

Age	Total Population		Severely Disabled	
Less than 1 year	409	6.9	2	2.1
1 to 5 years	1,359	22.9	38	39.5
6 to 10 years	1,744	29.4	33	34.4
11 to 15 years	1,626	27.4	18	18.8
16 to 21 years	795	13.4	5	5.2
Total	5,933	100.0%	96	100.0%
	Mean=10.5		Mean=7.8	

TABLE 4.2   Problems Presented by Severely Developmentally Disabled Children in Foster Home Care

Problem	N	%
Mental retardation	76	41.4
Seizure disorders	24	13.0
Cerebral palsy	18	9.8
Emotional problems	24	13.0
Blind	16	8.7
Deaf	4	2.2
Heart disorder	3	1.6
Other medical problems	19	10.3
Total	184	100.0%

Of particular relevance in this issue is that foster parents, social workers, other professionals and/or institutions have been the sources for the information relating to these problems. In comparing the sources for agreement, it was found that slightly over 56% agreed on the existence of the problem. In six cases, all the sources agreed on the identification of the problems except for the social worker. In another four cases, the social worker and the foster parent disagreed. It is a simple truism that such disagreement does not work in the best interests of a child.

Table 4.3 indicates the primary source of treatment for the children in this study. The largest group of children are actively involved in special education programs. Over half

TABLE 4.3 Types of Treatment, Implementation, and Recommendations Pertaining to Severely Developmentally Disabled Children in Foster Home Care

Treatment	Recommended and Implemented		Recommended but Not Implemented		Recommended and Implementation Pending	
	N	%	N	%	N	%
Surgical/medical	41	27.2	1	7.1	4	10.5
Physical/speech/ occupational therapy	36	23.8	6	42.9	9	23.7
Psychiatric	8	5.3	2	14.3	5	13.2
Special education	56	37.1	3	21.4	5	13.2
Residential	10	6.6	2	14.3	15	39.4
Total	151	100.0%	14	100.0%	38	100.0%

are attending special classes either for retarded, emotionally disturbed, or physically handicapped children.

Table 4.4 presents the data related to the length of time that children have been in treatment programs. Fifteen children have been in treatment for more than 5 years and 14 are expected to be continuous for the remainder of their lives. Those in the "more than 5 years" category generally are in special education programs. The children who can be expected to be in treatment for the remainder of their lives fall into the medical/surgical category.

With regard to the use of medication, it was found that 50% of the children were taking medicine for the control of seizures. Less than one-quarter of the children were taking psychoactive medications. One of the major problems cited in the course of this study was that some foster children did not receive their medicine because their foster parents refused to follow through with the medication treatment program. This was true for almost 12% of the children for whom anticonvulsant medicines were prescribed and 25% of the children for whom psychiatric medicines were prescribed. The foster parents offered no explanation for not administering the medicine except that they did not agree that the child needed it.

SOCIAL WORK SERVICES

As part of this study, social workers were asked to rate the foster parents according to their knowledge of the child's experiences. Almost 3/4 of the foster parents were rated good to excellent by the social workers. Table 4.5 indicates, however, that 13 foster parents, or pairs of foster parents, as the case may be, were given low ratings by the social worker. This fact is particularly troublesome when considering the degree of the child's disability and, therefore, his possible continued dependency.

TABLE 4.4 Length of Time the Severely Developmentally Disabled Children in Foster Home Care Have Been in Treatment

Type of Treatment	Less than 2 years N	Less than 2 years %	25 months to 5 years N	25 months to 5 years %	More than 5 years N	More than 5 years %	Continuous for life N	Continuous for life %
Surgical/medical	10	19.6	9	17.6	3	20.0	10	71.5
Physical/speech/ occupational therapy	11	21.6	18	35.3	0	----	2	14.3
Psychiatric	4	7.8	3	5.9	0	----	0	----
Special education	19	37.3	18	35.3	11	73.3	1	7.1
Residential	7	13.7	3	5.9	1	6.7	1	7.1
Total	51	100.0%	51	100.0%	15	100.0%	14	100.0%

TABLE 4.5   Ratings of Foster Parents of Severely Developmentally Disabled Children

Rating	N	%
Excellent	56	58.3
Good	14	14.6
Adequate--difficult child	7	7.3
Adequate	3	3.1
Inadequate--child needs to be institutionalized	1	1.0
Inadequate	2	2.1
Professionals disagree	7	7.3
No rating	6	6.3
Total	96	100.0%

Attention was also paid to the quality of the social worker's services. Frequency of contact with the foster family, foster parent's perception of the social worker, and social worker's familiarity with the case, as rated by the Project staff, were addressed.

Table 4.6 shows that 1/2 the social workers had direct contact with the foster family at least once a month but Table 4.7 shows that less than 1/3 of the social workers were considered to be helpful by the foster parents. According to the assessments of the Project staff, over 70%

TABLE 4.6 Frequency of Direct Social Worker Contact with Foster Parents of Severely Developmentally Disabled Children

Frequency	N	%
Once a month or more	48	50.0
Once each 2 to 3 months	25	26.1
Once each 6 months	4	4.2
Once each year	1	1.0
No contact	13	13.5
Don't know	5	5.2
Total	96	100.0%

TABLE 4.7 Foster Parent Rating of Social Workers of Severely Developmentally Disabled Children

Rating	N	%
Helpful	30	31.3
Somewhat helpful	2	2.1
Ambivalent	11	11.5
Negative, not enough contact	1	1.0
Negative, no help	3	3.1
Negative, no contact	17	17.7
Did not say	32	33.3
Total	96	100.0%

of the social workers had good to excellent knowledge of the cases (Table 4.8).

All of the individuals who were interviewed were asked if there were any specific problems in obtaining special services for the children in their care. The greatest number of complaints concerned securing services from hospitals and other institutions (37). Monetary problems ranked second in frequency (34).

The greatest difficulty reported with regard to hospitals and other institutions was that either facilities were not available or that long waiting lists prevailed. This problem is related to the monetary difficulties, however, in that lack of funds or over-restrictive use of funds renders assistance inaccessible.

Other problems encountered with the hospitals and other institutions were that personnel frequently failed to share professional information with foster parents. Foster parent requests for information were frequently reported to have been totally ignored or passed off with such statements as "you wouldn't understand" or "nothing can be done."

TABLE 4.8   Research Staff Rating of Knowledge of Social Worker of Severely Developmentally Disabled Child in Foster Home Care

Rating	N	%
Excellent	56	58.3
Good	15	15.6
Adequate	9	9.4
Limited	16	16.4
Total	96	100.0%

More specific difficulties regarding the monetary issues included refusal of professionals to treat the child (6), refusal for pharmaceutical services (10), domestic needs (7), and combinations of the above (9).

One-quarter of the parents are receiving no extra funds for the care of the severely developmentally disabled child in their home. Another 25% receive $20 or less per month in extra care funds. Nineteen receive between $21 and $40 per month, 6 receive $41 to $60 per month, and 16 receive more than $60 per month. It can be seen that there is great variation in the amount paid to foster parents for extra care, and this has no obvious correlation to any of the specifics of a child's case.

EXAMPLARS

There are a number of problems specifically related to a disabled child's placement in foster care. For very handicapped children, just being in foster home care further complicates an already extremely difficult situation. In order to illustrate some of these problems, these examplars are provided (as specific as confidentiality will allow). This has turned out to be no easy task in that information is incomplete on the vast majority of these children, and sometimes conflicts in terms of their problems and treatment needs. It is for this reason that most of the recommendations of this study are made in such a way as to apply to all children in foster home care in order to standardize information. In that way, the child who is identified as being developmentally disabled can much more likely be assured of receiving adequate services.

Many of the problems contained in these examples may be due to the confusing nature of the reported disabilities since professionals appear to be hesitant to label children as handicapped at early ages. Another possible explanation is that children in foster home care obviously get insufficient evaluation and treatment services. If a child waits to be placed in an institution, it may be to his or her advantage as the foster parent finds out that the child can appropriately respond to the home situation. On the other hand, as the child waits, the foster family may become more and more frustrated with the child, and this in itself can often be damaging.

One very important factor is the number of children who have not had an assigned social worker for a long period of time. In many instances, the foster parents have secured treatment and services by their own initiative, but have stated the definite need for a social worker to help in making referrals and in obtaining treatment for their foster child. There are other cases, however, where either the child receives no treatment or has it discontinued by the foster parents. This happens without consultation or the benefit of supervision from a staff member from the Division of Family and Children's Services.

The following case involves two children under the age of 3 years. The first child is a 2 1/2 year old female who was born with multiple congenital anomalies, severe congenital heart disease, gross mental and motor retardation, loss of hearing, and a partial loss of vision. Since birth, she has been hospitalized many times and has been evaluated and received treatment, both in the area where she resides and in several major Boston hospitals. Although her life expectancy is extremely limited, it has been stated by her physician that the foster mother extended this life expectancy by providing excellent care and treatment for this child. The family has received no assistance or referrals from the social worker. There has been no assigned social worker for this child and her family for at least 2 years which obviously covers the vast majority of her life. It is possible that the foster mother may need some help in the future when she must cope with the death of the child.

The second case is a 2 year old child with a congenital loss of the left eye and socket, impaired vision in her right eye, small head circumference, and delayed development in motor difficulties in the lower extremities. Some treatment has been implemented in the area of physical therapy with the help of the social worker from the Adoption Placement Unit. The foster mother states that, other than two visits from the adoption worker, she has not seen or heard from a social worker or the regional office since the child was placed in her home 2 years ago. The adoption worker has stated that she has been unsuccessful in her attempts to have a local ongoing social worker assigned to this case, and that she has not visited the home in 1 year.

As previously noted, there are some instances where the treatment has been discontinued without consultation or supervision from a social worker or other professional. The apparent lack of services is exemplified in the situation which exists for two children in one foster home.

These children have been in foster care for 4 1/2 years. One child has been in the present foster home for almost a year. The second child has lived there for almost 1 1/2 years. One and a half years ago, they were diagnosed by a specialist as having a seizure disorder with possible mental retardation. The medication was supposed to continue for at least 3 years, at which time periodic evaluations would determine the continued need for such medication. As stated by the specialist, the care of the children would be followed through by the local pediatrician. The foster mother would also continue with the daily medication. The specialist stated on the telephone that, depending on the frequency and severity of the seizures, there would be permanent health and mental damage if the medication were to be discontinued. He last evaluated one of the children 1 year ago, and the other 3 months after the initial diagnosis. He assumes they are presently receiving their medication and follow-up care with the pediatrician. The pediatrician involved, however, has never seen one of the children and has not seen the other since his referral to the specialist. He has no knowledge that she is still being seen by the specialist.

The original foster mother for these children has stated that they were attending special classes for the mentally retarded, and both received daily anticonvulsant medication. In addition, one child presented other medical problems and severe seizures, all of which required periodic evaluation. The current foster mother states that both of the children are perfectly normal and healthy, and therefore, she has removed them from the special classes and discontinued all medication and medical treatment since, at least in her view, it is not necessary.

Since this has been an uncovered case for at least 1 year, the Project staff contacted the previous social workers. They did not indicate to the staff that they had any knowledge of the present situation in the current foster home.

Of the 96 severely developmentally disabled children in this sample, as indicated previously, 18 currently had no social worker assigned even if the foster parent indicated the desire for one. In addition to this number, 29 were without a social worker for long periods of time before they were formally assigned one.

Several foster parents have stated their major problem in obtaining treatment for the children was the sporadic coverage and help of the social workers. In many cases, there was no social worker for at least 18 months. In other cases, there was only sporadic coverage for short periods of time. During the period that the child had no social worker, the foster parents often found it very difficult to obtain the necessary treatment for the child, and in a few cases, never obtained it at all.

A specific example involved a 10 year old severely retarded child. There was no social worker for at least 18 months. When one was finally assigned, the child was evaluated as being severely retarded and hyperactive with possible emotional disturbance. The child entered a special day school and then the case was again uncovered for a second period of 18 months. Although the child was in a special day school during this time, the foster mother had a great deal of difficulty attempting to control the problem behaviors, such as, setting fires, biting, and head banging which he displayed while at home. His present social worker was assigned to the case 7 months ago.

Another case is that of an adolescent boy who, for 9 years, was a resident of a state hospital where he received some medical treatment and attended special classes. He was discharged to his foster home in 1968 with the diagnosis of congenital encephalopathy, mental retardation, and spastic diplegia. In the beginning of 1972, he was evaluated again and sporadically seen for treatment at a public health clinic. For 1 year after this evaluation, there was no social worker for this child, and the foster parent often did not take him for physical therapy as recommended. A worker from the clinic made a home visit and the foster mother again started taking the adolescent for the prescribed treatments. Although the boy was attending special classes within the public school system during this time, the foster mother stated that she felt he needed a special school to receive vocational training. But she did not know how to accomplish this without a social worker. Recently the family moved to another part of the state and the foster parents are obtaining a divorce. The child is no longer in school or receiving physical therapy. It was recommended that he be placed in a residential school at this time. It is not known, however, if such placement procedures have been started.

There are a few cases where the physicians have stated that nothing can be done for the child. One such case is that of a 12 year old girl who is completely bedridden. According to her foster parent, she had never been thoroughly evaluated or received any treatment other than general pediatric services until very recently. This child was hospitalized at least once in the past. She has the appearance of a toddler. Information from the social worker and the foster mother states that this child is a spastic quadraplegic, has no speech, is completely blind, is microcephalic, with severe mental retardation. She must be fed only a diet of strained baby food. This child has been in this home since birth although the home has only recently been a licensed foster home.

In the past, the physicians would only say that she would die in early infancy. They further stated that there was absolutely nothing that would help the child. During the last few years when the foster mother was part of the Division of Family and Children's Services, she was refused services by hospitals, physicians, and pharmacies because this child was a "ward of the state." From the foster mother's viewpoint, no one seemed to care or be interested in helping this child until her current social worker was assigned a year ago. A complete evaluation is now in progress. A clinical nursery and a wheel chair have already been recommended as a possible part of the initial treatment.

In many instances, residential placement has been recommended for these particular children. But often there has either been an extremely long waiting list or no facilities available for residential care. The following children are two of the most severely disabled within the sample.

One special case is a 6 year old child with spastic quadraplegia and severe mental retardation. In addition, she is unable to chew food and must be fed with a bottle. This child is completely bedridden and is not able to do anything for herself. A pediatric nursing home had been recommended, but both the foster mother and the social worker state there is nothing available now and there exists a definite lack of facilities for this particular child.

One 10 year old girl had been diagnosed as having a seizure disorder, mild mental retardation, congenital encephalopathy, and emotional disturbance. It seems that no person is quite sure of her exact disabilities, and this has made it even more difficult to contend with. Because she is both mentally retarded and emotionally disturbed, this child was refused by one residential treatment facility and is currently on the waiting list for another. She has been refused out-patient services at a variety of facilities. Professionals state that treatment was available but could not be utilized because of the combination of the existing problems of this child. The foster parents state that they can no longer adequately deal with the situation. They feel that foster home care is no longer efficient and the child must enter a treatment facility. Neither the foster parents nor the social worker know what will be done to meet this child's needs if she is not accepted very soon at some treatment facility.

The lack of available treatment facilities is a substantial problem for children in foster home care who do not also require residential treatment. These facilities range from local treatment centers, clinics, and hospitals, to special nurseries, public education, and private physicians. In at least 12 cases, it was stated that no facilities were available or there were long waiting lists delaying the treatment program of the child. The apparent lack of services is exemplified in the following two cases.

One 6 year old has a rare syndrome in addition to being mentally retarded and emotionally disturbed. There is no specific data available for this syndrome and the child must travel to Boston since no facilities exist in his immediate area. This has created a transportation problem for the foster family and the social worker. Although he is attending a community clinical nursery, it has been recommended that he receive extra psychological and/or psychiatric help for his emotional problems. In this case, the social worker stated that there was a problem in getting accepted into a program because of his retardation. The social worker felt that foster children in general are discriminated against in the school system and in the state mental health clinics which should presumably be available to them.

The second child is 5 years old with severe emotional problems and limited vision in one eye. He's also had previous medical problems. His foster mother states that when he is not destroying things he will just sit motionless for many hours and stare into space. This child has been receiving treatment for his medical problems since birth, but until recently, it was felt it would be best to wait for a psychological evaluation because of the multiple number of hospitalizations and medical problems. Recently, however, when the foster mother and the social worker tried to obtain an evaluation and treatment at a local state mental health facility, they were refused since the facility stated that they did not take children, especially preschoolers. The social worker continued the attempt to arrange for this evaluation, but was referred back and forth between local clinics and different hospitals in Boston. During this time, the child was placed in another foster home which also delayed the evaluation. When the staff last contacted the social worker, attempts were still being made to arrange an evaluation at a Boston hospital since nothing was available in the immediate area where the child is living. It is not known if an evaluation was completed or any treatment was obtained.

It is often extremely difficult to obtain treatment for children where there are conflicting diagnoses of mental retardation and emotional disturbance.

The following case is that of a mentally retarded adolescent who is also confined to a wheel chair because of spastic quadraplegia. She only has limited use of one hand and her speech is severely affected. During a 4 year period, this child attended school for the first 2 years and underwent multiple orthopedic procedures at one particular hospital. During the second 2 years she received home tutoring. There has been no follow-up care or contact with this hospital in the last 5 years. The prognosis at this time was very poor, and the hospital said little could be done for her.

For 3 years after this treatment, the only follow-up care was provided by a visiting nurse and there was no schooling at all. Both the foster parent and the social worker feel that this hospital did not properly follow through. For the past 1 1/2 years, the adolescent has been receiving treatment from a regional mental health facility and has resumed classes in a special class for the handicapped last fall. The major problem that existed was the 3 year gap in treatment. The foster parent and social worker attribute this to the prognosis as stated by the hospital.

Another case involves a 5 year old child with severe mental retardation and a number of medical problems. He had been treated at a Boston hospital since birth until 2 years ago. The foster parents stated that the child was not receiving any schooling or treatment other than general pediatric services until he entered school earlier this year. The main problem, as stated by the social worker, was the difficulty he had in securing copies of the results and records of the evaluation and treatment from the hospital. It was felt by both the foster parent and social worker that this delayed obtaining a school setting for this child.

An example of the difficulties with physicians and other professionals is demonstrated by the following case. This child had been diagnosed as having cerebral palsy. The child's physician refused to refer him to a specialist or the local treatment facilities for cerebral palsy. Finally the social worker and foster parent together arranged to have an evaluation and referral to a Boston hospital. There was still a great deal of difficulty since the physician refused to send the necessary information to the cerebral palsy clinic.

From the time of evaluation and referral by the hospital until the child entered treatment at the clinic, there was a delay of over 8 months. Since this time, the foster family has prevented any possible similar future problems by obtaining the services of another physician.

An additional problem in obtaining treatment for the children was financial. Within the sample of 96 children, over 1/3 of the foster parents and social workers stated that treatment was refused because the children were "wards of the state" or that there were other financial difficulties for the foster parents to provide the necessities for the children from the limited amount of money they received from the Department of Public Welfare. The greatest percentage of this number said they were refused pharmaceutical services, and the only way they were able to secure the necessary medication or services was to pay for it themselves and then be reimbursed by the Commonwealth.

One such case is a 2 year old who is severely mentally retarded, bedridden, and has a seizure disorder. Daily medication for seizure control has been prescribed, but the foster mother states that some pharmacies refuse to accept the vouchers for payment or bill the Department for a child who is under their care. This foster parent further stated that the amount she received for the child from the Commonwealth was insufficient to meet all her needs, especially the clothing allowance.

A number of foster parents indicated that they have had administrative problems with the Division of Family and Children's Services. The most frequently stated problem was the fact that the foster parents were not advised beforehand about the children's specific difficulties or the previous evaluation and treatment which they may have received. In the case of one 3 1/2 year old child, the foster parents stated that they were given no idea about his problems before he came to their home. Because of this, the foster parents felt that people were trying to hide his background from them for some reason. They subsequently asked for him to be removed from their home for these reasons but then decided to keep him because of their commitment. In a few cases, the foster parents reported the same problems and also stated that had they known this information it would have been extremely beneficial for them in understanding and more adequately dealing with their children.

In summary, the previously related cases were only a few examples from the sample of 96 of the apparent lack of services and facilities for the severely developmentally disabled child in foster care. It is obvious from the data gathered in this study that, although many children are receiving needed services, there are many more who require additional services from providers of treatment, both in the private and public sectors. These children, however, continue to be seriously neglected by the very institutions and professionals who are charged with their care.

NOTES

1. Additional weight was given to these conditions as a consequence of the policies of the Massachusetts Bureau of Developmental Disabilities which funded a portion of the Project.

Chapter 5

THE BIOLOGICAL PARENTS

Parents selected for interviewing in this component of the study were chosen by random sample and, for the most part, were interviewed in their homes. Obtaining data from the parents proved to be one of the most difficult aspects of the project. Table 5.1 presents the reasons why the project staff could not obtain data from the majority of parents selected.

In spite of their access to Department of Public Welfare records, discussions with social workers, and tracking through the Post Office, the research staff could not locate more than 37% of the parents of children in foster home care. To a great extent, the children of these parents are those "orphans of the living" who are in foster home care and have been subsequently abandoned by their parents. These children are not free for adoption, are cared for totally by the Commonwealth, and in almost every case are devoid of any parental or other natural family contact.

**TABLE 5.1 Reasons for Inability to Interview Parents
of Children in Foster Home Care**

Reason	N	%
Whereabouts unknown	220	37.6
No response to request for interview	41	7.0
Out of state	33	5.6
Deceased	29	5.0
Requested by social worker not to interview due to "casework" reasons	26	4.4
No show, i.e., neither cancelled nor kept interview appointment	19	3.2
Refused to participate	18	3.1
Not able to interview due to mental illness	16	2.7
Not interviewed due to impending court action involving child's custody	10	1.7
Not able to interview due to physical illness	5	0.9
Other	9	1.5
Interviews completed	160	27.3
Total	586	100.0%

Given the above, it should be kept in mind that the data in this chapter are based upon the responses of parents who could be contacted. Since they represent less than 30% of the sample selected, these data should not be construed as representative of all parents but, rather, as considerably biased in a positive direction. Therefore, whatever conditions are presented herein are, in fact, considerably worse.

IDENTIFYING DATA

Of the parents interviewed for this component of the study, 18% were female. Their average age was 32.5 years. Of the 160 parents interviewed, 157 (98.1%) were biological and 3 (1.9%) were adoptive.

All parents were English-speaking. There were 13 (8.1%) who were foreign-born, and they had been in the United States for an average of almost 24 years.

Fifteen percent of the parents reported that they had been in foster home care themselves when they were children. The majority were there for longer than 1 year.

Consistent with the data collected on the children, the racial distribution of the parents was as follows: 84.4% were white, 11.9% were black, 1.2% were interracial and 1.9% felt that they were unable to identify themselves through the traditional categories. Racial identification for one parent was missing. There were no Oriental or Spanish-speaking parents in the sample.

Table 5.2 presents the data pertaining to the religious preference of the parents.

As can be seen from Table 5.3, almost 1/2 the parents are currently divorced or separated.

When comparing current marital status with marital status just prior to the child's placement, it can be seen that the categories of "separated" and "divorced" account for

TABLE 5.2 Religious Preference of Parents of Children in Foster Home Care

Religion	N	%
Catholic	93	58.1
Protestant	55	34.4
Jewish	1	0.6
None	8	5.0
Other	3	1.9
Total	160	100.0%

approximately 1/2 in each case. The fact that at the time of placement the "separated" category is greater than the "divorced" is undoubtedly the result of many of the parents separating prior to the time of the foster home placement and obtaining divorces while their child has been in care.

Table 5.3 indicates that 40% of the current marriages are intact, even though approximately 56% of them are second or subsequent marriages. It can be seen that there are dramatic changes in marital status in the "first marriage" and "second or subsequent marriage" categories. Again, much of this is accounted for by the passage of time.

Table 5.4 presents data which serve as an index of the socio-economic status of the parents of children who are in foster home care.

The socio-economic status of the majority of these families is lower working class. Over 3/4 have incomes of less than $5,000, and less than 1/2 report employment as their main source of income.

TABLE 5.3   Marital Status of Parents of Children in Foster Home Care*

Marital Status	N		%	
First marriage	28	(42)	17.5	(26.8)
Second or subsequent marriage	36	(14)	22.5	(8.9)
Single	6	(10)	3.8	(6.4)
Separated	36	(51)	22.5	(32.4)
Divorced	38	(27)	23.7	(17.2)
Widowed	16	(13)	10.0	(8.3)
Total	160	(157)	100.0%	(100.0%)

*Figures in parentheses refer to marital status just prior to their child's entrance into foster home care.

It is clear from these data that foster home care is a program primarily utilized by poor and near-poor people. The all-important question, of course, is, "Are the factors which prompt a family to place a child in foster home care the same as those that cause poverty?" Since the vast majority of people below poverty levels do not ever place their children in foster homes, it is likely that the answer to the above question is negative. The second question, then, is, "What are the resources which are available to those who are not poor and, obviously unavailable to the poor, which allow the former to maintain the integrity of their families?" The answer to that question is likely to be found in the inherent discrimination of the dichotomy between ser-vices provided by the private and public sectors. The poor receive services in hospital out-patient clinics, state mental health clinics, social agencies or, worse yet, do not receive them at all. The non-poor receive services primarily in the private arena. So long as health and welfare programs sus-tain that dichotomy, this situation will undoubtedly persist. The only conceivable and rational solution to this problem is to establish programs which will make high quality medi-cal, dental, mental health, education, vocational training, and social health care universally available. At the same time these programs will maintain at least minimal financial solvency for the family.

CHILDREN

The biological parents generally reported having between four and five children in the family, but the vast majority have no children living with them now. In 5% of the cases, the mother was pregnant at the time of the interview.

Less than one-quarter have more than two children at home. The average parent stated that she had more than three children in foster home care at some time in the past and almost all of them were still in care. Twenty percent of the parents stated that they have surrendered one or more children for adoption. Siblings of the child were placed at the same time in 63.1% of the cases. Children were placed in the same foster home 45% of the time. Only about 7% of the parents specifically did not want their children placed together in the same home.

Even with the questions of representativeness, as raised in the first section of this chapter, the data obtained describing the particular child focused on in this report reflected the data in Chapter Two. That is, the average age, racial/ethnic identification, length of time in foster care,

TABLE 5.4 Total Family Income, Occupation, and Education of Parents of Children in Foster Home Care

Total Family Income	N	%
Less than $3,000	59	36.9
$3,00 to $4,999	39	24.4
$5,000 to $6,999	24	15.0
$7,000 to $9,999	21	13.1
$10,000 to $14,999	7	4.4
$15,000 to $19,999	2	1.2
Don't know	8	5.0
Total	160	100.0%

****

Occupation	N	%
Housewife/unemployed by choice	56	35.1
Unemployed, not by choice	35	21.9
Sales, civil service, clerical, para-professional	23	14.4
Skilled labor	22	13.8
Unskilled labor	17	10.6
Student	2	1.2
Retired	2	1.2
Professional	1	0.6

Don't know	2	1.2
Total	160	100.0%

****

Education	N	%
Less than eighth grade	45	28.1
Some high school	66	41.3
High school or equivalent	32	20.0
Post high school/technical or trade	10	6.2
Some college	6	3.8
College graduate	1	0.6
Total	160	100.0%

and similar factors were all comparable to the average data obtained from the social workers on the entire population of children.

THE PLACEMENT

Although 91% of all of the children in foster home care in Massachusetts are in the care of the Department of Public Welfare, it was found that only 83.8% of the parents in the sample had placed their children with the Department of

Public Welfare. The differences in the proportion are due to the fact that most of the inaccessible parents were Department cases. As the sample continued to be selected, the Department cases were more likely to be rejected due to inaccessibility, while the private agency cases that appeared tended to be maintained. Hence, a larger number of private agency cases are included in this section than would ordinarily be expected on the basis of actual proportions of children in care.

The parents interviewed indicated that placement occurred through voluntary means 58.8% of the time. This compares with about 52% of the general foster home care population. Only eight children in this sample have been released for adoption subsequent to the placement. Their reasons for placing the child in foster home care are presented in Table 5.5.

Consistent with the data collected from the social workers, mental illness of a parent was the greatest single reason for placing a child in foster home care. Neglect or abuse follows second.

The reasons for the necessity of the child's placement in foster home care seem to fall into a number of general categories. The largest group, 35.6%, entered foster home care for problems which were not directly related to the child. For instance, the parent(s) was experiencing divorce, desertion, a jail sentence, etc. The second largest group, 25%, was attributed to such incapacitation of the parent(s) as mental or physical illness or hospitalization. Twelve percent of the children were placed because the parent(s) could not control the child's behavior and the remainder were placed for diverse reasons.

About 34% of the parents stated that the original decision to place the child in foster home care was theirs. Placement was the result of a judicial decision in about 1/4 of the cases, and the social worker was the greatest influence in 18.8%.

TABLE 5.5 Reasons Parents Stated That Their Children Were Placed in Foster Home Care

Reason for Placement	N	%
Mental illness of parent	27	16.9
Neglect or abuse	23	14.4
Physical illness of parent	19	11.9
Drug addiction or alcoholism	8	5.0
Child placed as part of treatment plan for emotional disturbance	8	5.0
Death of parent	7	4.4
Divorce or desertion	6	3.8
Parent doesn't know	6	3.8
Child ran away	3	1.9
Child referred for placement by juvenile court	3	1.9
Not able to decide to keep child or surrender for adoption	3	1.9
Parent(s) in jail	2	1.3
Surrendered for adoption	2	1.3
Other	43	26.5
Total	160	100.0%

Almost 2/3 of the parents stated that a specific crisis precipitated the need for the child's placement and these were related to the variety of reasons presented in Table 5.5. Most important is that many of the parents were unable to obtain appropriate professional assistance for the problems until the placement was the impending plan. Once the child was placed in the foster home, however, very little service is provided to the family. Consequently, 28.8% reported that their family situation has remained the same with respect to problems. Deterioration of the family was reported by 14.4% of the parents.

Three-quarters of the children were still in foster home care on the date that the parents were interviewed and, based upon the above, prognosis for return is rather bleak. It was reported that there is no longer any contact with the social worker in about half the cases of those children who had been returned to their parents. Since the data on the children were collected as of November 18, 1971, and the parent interviews took place during the second quarter of 1972, it is apparent that the child's return could not have occurred much sooner before the interview took place. In spite of the fact that those children who had been returned could only have been back home for a matter of a few months, at most only half the cases were being followed by a social worker.

In cases where the child had been in foster home care prior to the placement in question, the parent was asked whether or not she had seen a social worker during the interim. Again, about 1/2 the parents of children who had been placed more than once replied in the negative. It would appear to be a relatively safe assumption that if there were more adequate follow-up on discharged cases, then at least some of the subsequent placements might be avoided.

Almost 30% of the parents felt that, in retrospect, placing their child in foster homes was not necessary. About 10% were unsure about it. Of those parents, 25%

stated that they could not do otherwise at the time because of financial difficulties. Another 23.3% of the parents reported that they thought placement could have been avoided if they had been able to receive quicker or more intensive family counseling, and 16.7% thought that having a homemaker would have been all that was necessary. The remaining 35% of the parents responded with a variety of reasons for placing their children in foster home care.

According to the parents, there was almost no initial consideration of options to the necessity of the child going into foster home care. Homemakers were discussed in about 3% of the cases. Day care was only talked about in less than 2% and other child care arrangements in 2.5%. This was in spite of the fact that 28.8% of the parents felt that accessibility to day care alone would have been enough to make a substantial difference in the decision.

The parents were asked about their perception of whether or not they were given a realistic picture of foster home care by the social worker prior to the placement. Twenty percent stated that they were not. Of considerably greater concern, however, is the fact that 42.5% of the parents reported that it was not talked about at all. Only 18% met the foster parents before the placement. This appears to indicate that there is not enough adequate pre-placement work in the majority of cases, once again probably due, in part, to the short staff and heavy caseload situation.

When the parents were asked about whether or not their child agreed with the necessity of a foster home placement, almost half the children were said to be too young to understand the issues. However, 27.9% of the children were against the plan and an equal proportion were either in favor from the beginning or eventually adjusted to the idea. According to the parents, 19% of the children did not really understand what was happening and about 20% of the children were "pressured" into entering care. Of the parents, 25.3% did not know how the child felt. In any event, over 60% of the parents stated that they felt as if they were excluded from participating in the process with their children when it came to dealing with their reactions.

Sixty percent of the parents do not know how long they can expect their child to be in a foster home. About 12% are considering releasing the child for adoption but have not been able to resolve the question to implement their decision.

Twenty percent of the parents think that the decision regarding their child's return home is entirely the social worker's. About 15% think that the child will be returned anytime they decide to accept him or her. Approximately 16% believe the decision to be up to the court and the remaining parents report that they understand that the decision will rest with a combination of people.

Over half the parents were vehement about their feelings that they would never again place a child in foster home care, and an additional 17% were ambivalent about it. About 1/4 of the parents felt that they would place one of their children again if the necessity arose again.

PARENT–CHILD CONTACT DURING PLACEMENT

It must be remembered that only 5% of the sample (eight children) have been released for adoption. All others remain in the custody of their parents. It must also be remembered that the parents in this section have much greater contact with their children in foster home care than is the case for the population at large. With this in mind, the parents were asked how often they saw their child while he was in foster home care. As can be seen from Table 5.6, more than 1/4 of the parents reported that there was no contact at all.

TABLE 5.6 Frequency of Parent–Child Contact, as Reported by Biological Parent, While Child Is in Foster Home Care

Frequency of Contact	N	%
Once a week or more	26	16.3
Once every other week	22	13.8
Once a month	28	17.5
Less than once a month	16	10.0
Varies greatly	26	16.2
Never	42	26.2
Total	160	100.0%

It is interesting that although these parents were the ones available for interviewing, they had a greater frequency of no contact with their child than the social workers reported for the entire population. Based upon the facts presented at the beginning of this chapter, one would more naturally assume that these parents would have more contact with their children than would be expected on the average. There are two possible explanations for the discrepancy. First, these parents may have adjusted better to the idea of having surrendered their children and are, therefore, quite open about the fact; whereas, the parents who were not available may still be avoiding the issues. Second, the social workers' estimates of frequency of parent–child contact as presented in Chapter Two may be too high, thereby indicating their lack of knowledge about parent involvement in their cases. The latter is more likely.

Of the parents who report contact with their children, 35.7% state that their contact is in their own home and about the same number, 34.8%, report that their visits are at the child's foster home. Less than 5% of the parents see their children at the agency. The remainder visit their children either at a combination of the places mentioned or on some completely neutral ground, such as the zoo or a movie.

About 70% of the parents who see their children in foster home care report that their visits usually vary in length from about an hour to an entire morning or afternoon. Another 15% report that the time varies, and the remainder state that visits are generally during school vacations, overnight, or weekends.

Of those parents who report contact, 36.2% stated that the social worker determined the times and places for the visits while 31% of the parents made the arrangements themselves. Almost 9% of the respondents stated that arrangements are made by the foster parent and the remainder were dictated by a combination of people.

With respect to the amount of time the parent spends with the child on each visit, 35% of the parents reported that the determination was made by the social worker. About 26% of the parents make that decision alone, and in almost 12% of the cases, it is left up to the foster parents. The child is in control of the length of the parental visits in about 5%. Only 3% are determined by the court. The remainder are decided by combinations of people.

Approximately 30% were happy with the frequency of their visits and 4% felt that they see the child too often. Yet about 60% of the parents felt that they do not see their child enough.

The parents who indicated that they do not have enough contact with their children were asked for the reasons which explain their inability to do so. Table 5.7 presents the distribution of those reasons.

TABLE 5.7   Reasons Given by Biological Parents of Children in Foster Home Care for Not Seeing Their Child as Much as They Would Like

Reason	N	%
Social worker says that contact is inappropriate	35	37.5
Personal schedule makes it too difficult	21	22.6
Foster parents do not like parent-child contact	18	19.4
Foster home is too far from parent	14	15.1
Foster home is too inconvenient to get to	5	5.4
Total	93	100.0%

It can be seen from Table 5.7 that 37.5% of the parents are prohibited from seeing their child as often as they wish, if at all, by the social worker. Though it is probably true that conceivably there are some reasons which might justify prohibiting parent–child contact, there is little question that it would not even begin to approach this proportion of the cases. Table 5.7, and especially this item, implies that the social workers often seem to be inhibiting the very changes they theoretically are attempting to bring about by working with the family.

Of even greater concern is that almost 20% of the parents state that parent–child contact is discouraged by the foster parent. Both of these situations are generally justified by positing that the child is "upset" by the move to the foster home, and visits from the natural parent(s) make it hard for the foster parent to deal with him. The fact that one of the prime objectives in many of these cases is to reunite the family seems to be ignored. There appear to be too many cases where parent–child contact is discouraged, and often prohibited, so as to protect the foster parent. It must be remembered, however, that the object of foster home care is to resolve the problems that forced placement and to eventually return the child to his biological family. Allowing the parent and child to become well-adjusted to foster home care may not be in the best interests of the child. Any intervening practice which, even temporarily, fails to direct foster home care toward returning the child home is a disservice. Foster care policy should necessitate consistent and frequent parent–child contact if the parent is to maintain legal rights.

It can also be seen that the distance from the parent's home to the foster home and the difficulty in getting there account for approximately 20% of the factors which inhibit parent–child contact. There does not seem to be enough emphasis on the necessity of the contact in order to maintain or improve the parent–child relationship. These data tend to support the implicit belief that foster home care is often, in itself, a terminal program. Once the child enters care, he simply remains there until he reaches majority.

PARENT–SOCIAL WORKER CONTACT

Table 5.8 shows that the majority of parents only have minimal contact with social workers from the agency supervising their childrens' placements. It can be seen that 31.2% of the parents never see a social worker at all, and even when that figure is adjusted to exclude the eight cases where the child has been released for adoption, it is unjustifiably high.

**TABLE 5.8   Frequency of Biological Parent's Contact
With Social Worker from Foster Home Care Agency**

Frequency of Contact	N	%
Regularly, every week or 2	40	25.0
Regularly, once a month	24	15.0
Once every 2 or 3 months	5	3.1
Less than every 6 months	19	11.9
When crises occur	14	8.8
When necessary, as like to foster parents	7	4.4
Never	50	31.2
Don't know	1	0.6
Total	160	100.0%

It must be remembered that about 16% of the parents in this sample have placed their children in foster home care with a private agency. In the private sector, uncovered and overloaded caseloads are the exception, rather than the rule. It can, therefore, be safely assumed that the majority of cases in Table 5.8, where there is minimal or no parent–social worker contact, are children placed with the Department of Public Welfare.

When the staff of any organization must function with approximately 1/3 less than its normal complement, statistics as reflected in Table 5.8 are to be expected. The social workers are constantly responding to crises and simply do not have the time to spend on cases where overt problems are not being presented. The consequences are that almost 60% of the families are not seen by the social worker within a 6 month period. Such infrequent contact is tantamount to a decision that the child will remain in foster home care until he reaches majority. This is certainly a breach of the initial contract under which the child was usually placed.

Infrequent parent–social worker contact is of considerable concern from the perspective of prevention of placement. When the parents were asked about their relationship with the foster care agency prior to the placement, it was discovered that 59.1% were in contact with the agency for 2 weeks or less. Over 3/4 of the parents had been in contact with the agency less than 3 months prior to the time the placement occurred. Eighty-two percent of the parents only saw their social worker six times or less before the child left home. Though this can be construed as a quick response to the need for foster home care, it is probably more accurate to say that once someone has made the referral, there is very little effort made by the agency to avoid the placement. Again, if a staff is severely undermanned, they obviously cannot have the necessary time to investigate viable alternatives with a family.

Of the parents who see the social workers now, it was reported that in about 39% of the cases their discussions generally concentrate on the child's progress or problems. Less than 18% of the parents reported that their discussions mainly focus on the family as a whole and 6.5% stated that they generally talk about their own problems. About 1/4 of the parents stated that discussions center around combinations of issues.

Even though only eight children (5%) have been released for adoption, as stated earlier, when the biological parents were asked if they thought enough was being done to help the family to be reunited, 16.9% (27) stated that they do not intend to take the child back home. Only 28.8%

of the parents answered in the affirmative and almost 40% in the negative. Over 13% of the parents were ambivalent about the issue. For example, some parents just could not decide whether enough was being done to bring their family together again.

The parents were rather negative in their perception of the social worker's desire to reunite the family. Only 11.2% of the parents felt that the social worker wanted to get the child back home as soon as possible. An additional 13.8% felt that the social worker wanted the child returned but at some future time. The remaining 3/4 of the parents reported that the social workers were either doubtful about the return of the child or clearly against it. Only about 30% of the parents agreed with the social worker's view.

Related to the issue of parent–social worker contact is the contact between the biological parents and the child's foster parents. There is absolutely no contact in about 40% of the cases. About 20% of the parents talk to the foster parents every week and an additional 23.1% do so once a month or more. The remaining parents only have infrequent contacts. The foster parents initiate the contact, at least sometimes, in about 1/3 of the cases.

DISCHARGED CHILDREN

Within the sample of 160, 21 children in care on November 18, 1971, had been returned to their parents by the time the interviews took place. They had been back home anywhere between 2 weeks and 5 months, with an average of about 1 month. The parents reported that they felt that foster care had brought about positive change in 11 of the cases, i.e., better parent–child relations and better relationships with other family members. Three children were reported as worse and four as exhibiting no changes since entering care.

CONCLUSION

Consistent with other data in this study, this chapter reinforces the idea that foster home care placement is a terminal goal in most cases. Though at the outset there is an implicit contract between the foster care agency and the family that services will be provided to resolve the problems leading to the placement, those services are frequently never brought to bear, and the child is simply maintained in a custodial setting—albeit usually better than the one he or she had left.

Once placement actually occurs, the biological parent appears to become secondary. Contact with the agency is minimal and parent–child contact is seldom encouraged and often discouraged.

In all, from the perspective of the biological parents, there is scanty evidence to suggest that the foster home placement that has been implemented for their child lives up to even minimal expectations.

Chapter 6

FOSTER PARENTS

In Chapter 5 it was noted that the research staff had considerable difficulty in locating and interviewing the biological parents of the children in foster home care. At certain points in this study data on a particular child have been combined with data gathered from his natural parents and his foster parents. As a result, the only foster parents who were interviewed were those who care for the children whose biological parents were contacted. Although that constitutes a biased sample, there is no reason to assume that these data still can't be generalized since the stability of the biological parents should not affect the decision regarding with which foster parent the child is actually placed.

One hundred forty-seven foster parents of children whose biological parents had previously been interviewed were included in this part of the study. All foster parents were seen in their home, as were the natural parents. These particular foster parents provide foster home care for 8% of the foster children in Massachusetts. Table 6.1 presents the distribution of numbers of children in these 147 foster homes.

TABLE 6.1 Distribution of Children in Foster Home Care

Number of Children in the Foster Home on Interview Date	N	%
1	45	30.7
2	30	20.4
3	18	12.2
4	18	12.2
5	10	6.8
6	8	5.4
7	3	2.0
8	2	1.4
9	6	4.1
10	2	1.4
11	1	0.7
16	1	0.7
19	3	2.0
Total	147	100.0%

On the target date four foster parents were interviewed about more than one child in their home but none with more than three children in their home were interviewed. An important point in this table is the number of children in each home. Department policy states that no more than six children under the age of 16, including the foster parents' biological children, shall be allowed in a foster home. The research staff selected a random sample of foster homes and discovered that 16% of the children were placed in homes where there were more than six children under the age of 16. These data indicate, therefore, that approximately 20% of the foster homes are overcrowded as defined by Department policy. There was no incidence of homes which contained more than two children under 2 years old, the second major criterion of Department policy dealing with overcrowding.

Of the foster parents interviewed, 10 (7%) were under private agency auspices and 137 (93%) were employed by the Department of Public Welfare. As stated in Chapter 2, approximately 2/3 of the children under private agency supervision are financially supported by the Department. Thus, it can be assumed that only three foster parents are not subsidized by the Department either directly or indirectly.

There are specific written policies about the requirements of foster homes for both the public and private sector. The Commomwealth provides guidelines for the private agencies and licenses these agencies to provide foster home care.[1]

IDENTIFYING INFORMATION

Of the 147 foster mothers interviewed, all were English-speaking and all but 7 mothers were born in the United States. Of the 7 who were foreign born 5 had been in the

United States over 19 years, 1 had been here for 5 years, and 1 for 7 years. The mean age of foster mothers as found in Table 6.2 was 45.7 years.

There was a foster father present in over 80% of the homes, his mean age was 46.4 years. One foster father was

TABLE 6.2   Ages of Foster Mothers

Age	N	%
20–24	2	1.4
25–29	12	8.2
30–34	23	15.6
35–39	13	8.9
40–44	31	20.9
45–49	18	12.3
50–54	14	9.5
55–59	16	10.9
60–64	8	5.4
65–69	3	2.1
70–74	4	2.7
75–79	2	1.4
Don't know	1	.7
Total	147	100.0%

not English-speaking. Six foster fathers were foreign-born, but each one had been in the United States for over 16 years.

Eighty-one percent of the foster mothers were presently married. Of the remaining foster mothers, 7 (4.8%) were separated, 12 (8.2%) were widowed, and five (3.4%) were divorced. There were 4 foster mothers (2.7%) who reported their marital status as single. As expected, there is significant difference in the percentage of married foster parents (81%) and married biological parents (40%). The frequency of single parent homes at less than 3% of foster parents and approximately 4% of biological parents is similar. Major differences appear in the frequency of foster parent separations and biological parent separation. This difference is maintained in the divorced category.

The racial/ethnic distribution of the 147 foster parents presented in Table 6.3 is consistent with the racial/ethnic distribution of the biological parents and the foster children.

About 8% of the children were placed with interracial parents. In the same sample, all black foster children were placed with black foster parents with one exception, a black child placed with a foster parent identified as interracial. One white child was placed with black foster parents, one with some other of nonspecified racial/ethnic background, four with interracial foster parents, and the remainder with white foster parents. Of the interracial children, three were in white homes, one in an interracial home, and one in a black home. Of the six "other" children, three were placed with white foster parents, two with black foster parents, and one with foster parents of unidentified race.

The study used income, education, and occupation as indicators of the socio-economic status of the foster parents. The data on these variables are presented in Table 6.4. They clearly indicate that most foster parents are working class, most typically earning between $7,000 and

TABLE 6.3 Racial/Ethnic Identification of Foster Parents

Race/Ethnicity	Foster Mothers		Foster Fathers	
	N	%	N	%
White	120	81.6	100	80.0
Black	23	15.7	18	14.4
Other	2	1.4	4	3.2
American Indian	0	0.0	2	1.6
Interracial	1	0.7	1	0.8
Spanish-speaking	1	0.7	0	0.0
Oriental	0	0.0	0	0.0
Total	147	100.0%	125	100.0%

$10,000 per year, high school-educated, and employed in a skilled trade.

Although both the foster and biological parents are of the same general socio-economic status, i.e., working class, there are substantial intragroup differences. If the data in Table 5.4 are compared with those in Table 6.4 one notes that in certain areas there are inverse proportions. Almost 37% of the biological parents earn less than $3,000 a year and an additional 24.4% earn between $3,000 and $4,999. This is compared with only 8.8% of the foster parents in the first category and 6.8% in the second. In other words, whereas 61.3% of the biological parents earn less than $5,000 a year, only 15.6% of the foster parents are found to be at that income level. As expected, the relationships at

the upper income levels are also reversed, i.e., only 5.6%
of the biological parents earn $10,000 or more compared
with 33.4% of the foster parents.

It is important to keep in mind that the foster parent
is reimbursed for some of the expenses related to care of
the child. But the natural parent, unless he is among the
40% reporting public assistance as main source of income,
receives no additional funds for support of the child. In
most cases, having the child at home puts the biological
parent under increased economic pressure and it can be
assumed that frequently the increased financial stress ei-

TABLE 6.4   Total Family Income, Occupation, and
Education of Foster Parents

Total Income	Income* N	%
Under $3,000	13	8.8
$3,000--$4,999	10	6.8
$5,000--$6,999	22	15.0
$7,000--$9,999	47	32.0
$10,000--$14,999	35	23.8
$15,000--$19,999	12	8.2
$20,000 or more	2	1.4
No answer	6	4.0
Total	147	100.0%

*Income does not include payments connected with
the care of foster children.

TABLE 6.4 continued

Occupation

Foster Father's Occupational Level	N	%	Foster Mother's Occupational Level	N	%
Unemployed by choice*	0	0.0			
Unemployed but not by choice*	3	2.0			
Student*	1	.7			
Unskilled	13	8.8	Unskilled	10	6.8
Skilled	57	38.9	Skilled	1	.7
Sales, Civil Service, etc.	34	23.1	Sales, Civil Service, etc.	23	14.3
Professional	9	6.1	Professional	3	2.0.
Retired*	9	6.1	Not working	0	0.0
Non-applicable	21	14.3	Non-applicable	112	76.2

Total   147   100.0%   Total   147   100.0%

*These categories were offered only on the foster father's occupational level and were not offered for the foster mother.

Education*

Years of Schooling	N	%
No formal schooling	2	1.4
Grades 1 through 4	0	0.0
Grades 5 through 8	21	14.3
Some high school	53	35.9
High school graduate or equivalency	46	31.3
Post high school/trade training	7	4.8
Some college	10	6.8
College degree	4	2.7

TABLE 6.4 continued

Total   147   100.0%

*Educational information was only available for foster mothers.

ther contributed to the child's placement or prevents his return. One of the most serious problems associated with the placement process is that often even though the removal of a child from his home alleviates at least some family financial stress it also militates against his return. The financial stress increases again if the biological parents accept the child back home. The disincentive for restoration of the biological family is, therefore, obvious.

The increased income margin may well be that additional factor which allows for purchasing of a home or establishing roots. These, in turn, are probably some of the factors which give the foster parents substantially greater ability to cope with stress than the biological parents.

Over 86% of the foster parents reported that they own their homes. Related to this fact is that the mobility of the foster parent population over the past 5 years is quite low. Over 70% of the families have not moved in 5 years. An additional 20% have moved only once and only two families have moved more than three times.

According to the foster parents, neighborhoods in which the majority of foster children are currently placed are different from the neighborhoods which they originally lived in. Table 6.5 presents the foster parents' perception of this.

This perception was reinforced when foster parents were asked if there were other foster parents in their community and if they knew of any families in their community who had placed their own children in foster home care. Only one foster mother in the sample had ever placed any of her own children in foster home care. Eleven percent of the foster parents knew a family in their community who had placed children in foster home care. In contrast to this, more than 2/3 were acquainted with other foster parents in their community.

Each foster mother was asked about neighbors', attitudes toward the idea of her being a foster parent. They

TABLE 6.5 Foster Parents' Perception of the
Comparative Similarity of Their Community and the
Community in Which the Foster Child Spent Most of
His Life

Degree of Similarity	N	%
Same community	18	12.2
Different community but similar in make-up and structure	10	6.8
Different	19	12.9
Very different	64	43.6
Don't know	19	12.9
Not applicable/infant placement	11	7.5
Not applicable/child lived mainly with foster parent	6	4.1
Total	147	100.0%

were also asked about their perception of how their neighbors felt about the specific child in her care. These data are presented in Table 6.6.

Neighbors seem to be more positive toward the foster child than they are of the idea of foster parenting. In both instances, however, it can be seen that there are comparatively few negative attitudes in the community. In fact, almost 3/4 of the foster children are reported to have friends in the immediate community. Thirteen percent of the foster children, however, who are old enough to have friends are reported to have none at all or very few. Some foster

TABLE 6.6 Foster Mothers' Perception of Their Neighbors' Acceptance of Foster Children and Acceptance of Their Role as a Foster Parent

Neighbors Feelings Towards Foster Mothering	N	%
Positive	88	59.9
Negative	3	2.0
Ambivalent	10	6.8
No special feelings	21	14.3
Don't know	25	17.0
Total	147	100.0%

Neighbors Feelings Toward Foster Child	N	%
Positive	104	70.8
Negative	4	2.7
Ambivalent	10	6.8
No special feelings	18	12.2
Don't know	11	7.5
Total	147	100.0%

parents complained of children being used as scapegoats in the community because, as one foster parent put it, "their own parents don't want them."

The interviews with foster parents took place about 6 months after the social workers collected data. Of the 147 foster children in the sample, 72.1% were still living in the foster home at the time of the interview and about 28% had left that home. The placements of the majority of foster children had lasted at least 6 months in the same foster home. Since 1969, or for at least 2 years, 45% of the sample children had been in this foster home. On the other hand, according to the foster mother, slightly more than 1/2 of the children had been in other foster home care placements prior to entering this one. This is well above the proportion of children in the overall study since 50% were reported by their social workers to have had only a single placement.

THE CHILDREN IN THEIR HOME

What does a foster mother know about the child she is to provide surrogate care for on the average of 4 1/2 years? What does she think this child's future should hold? What kind of service does she feel is needed and what does the child get?

In Chapter 2 it was indicated that 56.5% of the children in foster home care were placed on a voluntary or temporary basis. In Table 6.7 it is shown that foster mothers understood that only 33.3% of these children were expected to be temporarily placed. In fact, 12% (18) of the children were reportedly placed with specific time limitations. Of those 18 children, 10 were to stay less than 3 weeks, 4 were to stay 11 to 14 weeks, and 3 were to remain between 26 and 40 weeks. The average expected stay was computed to be slightly more than 9 weeks. It was discovered, however, that thus far they have actually been in

TABLE 6.7   **Expected Length of Stay in Foster Home Care**

Expected Length of Stay	N	%
Limited to specified date	18	12.2
Meant to be temporary but no exact time specified	31	21.1
Until child is self-supporting (or until 21 years old)	7	4.8
No limit	90	61.2
Don't know	1	0.7
Total	147	100.0%

foster home care for an average of approximately 3 1/2 years. Only one child was discharged from care as planned. The only immediate explanation for this discrepancy, especially when it is remembered that this sample is based upon the more stable biological families, is the lack of social work services which are provided for the children and their biological parents once placement occurs.

Table 6.8 presents interesting comparative information with Table 6.7 as the foster mothers reveal their more current expectations. The marked increase appears in the "Permanently" category in Table 6.8 as well as the category of "Planning to Adopt." These data seem to demonstrate that foster parents are not given a reliable expectation of how long the child will be with them. They may also indicate the frequency with which children could be restored to their biological parents if greater effort were expended in that direction.

TABLE 6.8   Foster Mothers' Current Anticipation of Child's Length of Stay

Length of Stay	N	%
Specified number of weeks	11	7.5
Don't know	47	32.0
Permanently	38	25.8
Planning to adopt	10	6.8
Child already left	41	27.9
Total	147	100.0%

Foster parents seldom meet the foster child prior to his placement in their home. Only 36% of the foster mothers and their foster children had been afforded such an opportunity. An even smaller number, slightly less than 18% of the foster parents had met the biological parents prior to the placement. This is the case in spite of the fact that 2/3 of the children were living with one or both parents prior to entering foster home care.

Foster parents knew or at least had some idea of why the child was entering foster home care in 72% of the cases. In 12.2% of the cases, however, the child's social worker had not spoken with the foster mother prior to the placement except to enquire about space availability.

Ninety-two children placed in the homes of the foster parents in this sample had some special need at the time of placement. In preparing for a foster placement it is crucial that the foster mother has complete knowledge of such problems. In Table 6.9, however, the data indicate that 3/4 of the parents were unaware of the child's special needs or did not realize the extent of the child's needs prior to his entering the foster home. This situation is as unfair to the foster parents as it is to the foster child. In many cases, unless that child's special need is quite visible, it means that he simply will not receive the proper services. This situation is virtually impossible to justify.

Table 6.10 presents the distribution of problems evidenced in the children who were reported to be handicapped in some way. There were 84 children who presented 137 different handicapping conditions. Of these 84 children, only 23.2% were known by their foster mothers to have had these problems evaluated prior to entering their care. In 12% of the cases, the foster mothers were unsure whether the problems had been evaluated, and at the time of the interview about 13% of the children's problems still remained unevaluated.

The reasons presented for the delays in obtaining the necessary services for the child are presented in Table 6.11.

TABLE 6.9   Foster Parents' Knowledge of Child's Special Needs

Information Supplied	N	%
Yes	23	25.0
Foster parent had some idea, but did not know extent of difficulties	25	27.2
No	44	47.8
Total	92	100.0%

TABLE 6.10 Type and Frequency of Disabilities Reported by Foster Parents Among Children in Their Care

Type of Disability	N	%
Intellectual	26	18.9
Behavior/emotional	23	16.8
Other medical problem	18	13.1
Toilet training	16	11.7
Speech	12	8.8
Physical disfigurement	11	8.0
Arm-hand use	9	6.6
Vision	8	5.8
Leg-foot use	6	4.4
Hearing	5	3.7
Convulsive disorder	3	2.2
Total	137	100.0%

The first part of the table addresses evaluation and the latter, treatment. The highest proportion of known delays in both instances are due to agency issues. These may be the most difficult to justify since they generally stem from bureaucratic factors. However small the numbers in the "Nonacceptance of Medicaid" category, the inherent injustice of the payment system is underscored as it apparently does deprive a number of children of necessary care and treatment. This point was addressed in Chapter 2, but it is important to emphasize that this may mean that up to 100 children or more are adversely affected. There are multiple reasons for children being deprived of services, but when agency delays become the obstacles, the foster care process seems to have reversed its role and function.

As tentatively proposed in Chapter 2, should foster parents be delegated greater responsibility for the foster children, it would become increasingly important that information about these children be shared to a much greater degree than it is at present. Although Table 6.12 indicates a low frequency of social work contacts with the foster homes, 72.6% of the foster mothers feel that the social workers are available as needed most of the time. The remaining foster mothers feel social workers are not readily available to them and, therefore, they are left with the immense responsibility of caring for a child, not their own, without Department support.

THE FOSTER PARENT ROLE

Each foster mother was asked to designate the reasons which led them to consider becoming a foster parent. The most frequent single response, given by about 60% of the respondents, was that they wanted to work with children. An equal number of foster parents stated that their awareness of the need for good foster homes was also an important part of their consideration. Less frequently mentioned reasons were that they knew a child who had entered foster care (10.2%); they had been foster children themselves (5.4%); and financial reasons (3.4%). Perhaps the most important aspect of this information is that very few people became foster parents solely for money, though it may be that only a few foster parents will admit to that reason.

TABLE 6.11 Problems Encountered in Getting Evaluations for Foster Child's Disability

Problem	N	%
Non-acceptance of Medicaid	2	2.4
Facilities too far away	4	4.8
Over-crowded facilities	2	2.4
Child's resistance to evaluation	0	0.0
Biological parents' resistance to evaluation	1	1.2
Foster care agency delays	11	13.1
Other	20	23.8
No delays	40	47.5
Don't know	4	4.8
Total	84	100.0%

***

Problem	N	%
Non-acceptance of Medicaid	2	2.4
Facilities too far away	2	2.4
Over-crowded facilities	3	3.6
No facilities	1	1.2
Child's resistance to treatment	1	1.2

Biological parents' resistance to treatment	0	0.0
Inability to get child to facilities	1	1.2
Foster care agency delays	10	11.9
Agency can't pay	3	3.6
Other	18	21.4
No delays	43	51.2
Total	84	100.0%

There are obviously a whole series of complex reasons which contribute to the decision to take on such serious responsibility. The community should in turn assume the responsibility to provide the foster parent with adequate payment and resources to do the job effectively.

Less than 1/4 of the foster parents received any training prior to becoming foster parents. Since taking on this responsibility however, about 46% of the mothers state they have been involved in activities to help them become better foster parents. Most of the foster mothers however, were self-motivated to do so, rather than required by the agency. Forty percent of the foster parents stated that they would be interested in more training related to their roles and responsibilities as a foster parent.

The very low frequency of financial motivation for becoming a foster parent is borne out in the data regarding expenses in raising foster children. More than 93% of the foster mothers state that they regularly must use their own financial resources to cover expenses for their foster chil-

TABLE 6.12 Frequency of Child's Social Worker Contacts With Child's Foster Mother

Frequency	N	%
Weekly	18	12.2
Few times a month	14	9.5
As need arises	50	33.9
Once a month	17	11.6
Every two/three months	22	15.0
Twice a year	7	4.8
Less than twice a year	12	8.2
Never after placement started started	7	4.8
Total	147	100.0%

dren. These are primarily reimburseable expenses, but the Department's reimbursement process is reported to be barely manageable in most instances. Since it is known that on the whole foster families have working class incomes, the extra expenditures for them in the foster care process are not a small matter. It would almost seem that the Department's constant pressure to account for and limit its expenditures has created serious financial handicaps for the foster parents. See Table 6.13.

When asked what they felt it would take to get others interested in foster parenting, multiple methods were suggested for recruitment. The most frequent suggestion was to increase publicity and public awareness of the need for foster parents. This was mentioned by 58.5% of the respondents. Almost half of the foster parents, however, felt that the most important single necessary change was to make better services available to them. The third most frequent response was to allot more money per child, again, mentioned by almost half of the parents. This response was made in spite of the fact that most foster parents previously mentioned that finances was not a consideration when deciding to become a foster parent. Related to this, about 1/3 of the foster parents thought salaries for foster parenting would interest more people.

TABLE 6.13   Assessment of the Financial Reimbursement Process in Foster Home Care

Foster Mother's Assessment	N	%
Convenient	31	21.1
Just manageable	14	9.5
Difficulty	58	39.4
Never got money back	9	6.1
Haven't tried yet	33	22.5
Not applicable	2	1.4
Total	147	100.0%

NOTES

1. See Appendix IV A for the Massachusetts Department of Public Welfare's guidelines pertaining to licensing of foster homes. Since the time of the study, licensing functions have been transferred to the Massachusetts Office for Children.

Chapter 7

SUMMARY AND RECOMMENDATIONS

GENERAL FINDINGS AND CONCLUSIONS

Over the last few years the nature of foster home care has changed considerably. For one thing, the children being placed now are generally much older than those placed in the past. Since foster care is increasingly utilized as an alternative to institutionalization, the frequency of placing severely disturbed and delinquent children is much greater. As a consequence, the demands upon the public and private child care agencies are different. To a great extent, some of the problems identified in this report can be attributed to those changes and the inability of agencies to adjust to the new demands.

The problems identified in this report can be divided into five categories.

1. Keeping Families Together

Virtually no effort is made to keep the biological family together and to prevent children from being placed into foster care.

There were 82% of the parents who saw a social worker six times or less before the placement, and 60% who were in contact with the foster care agency 2 weeks or less before the child was removed from home. In addition, it was shown that 23% of the children are placed in foster homes as a result of the mental illness of a parent. This indicates the lack of community-based services available to the disturbed parent who still maintains a child in his own home. Finally, though many of the parents felt that services such as day care, counseling, and homemakers would have made placement unnecessary, the Division of Family and Children's Services has only minimal ability to provide them.

Despite the temporary purpose of foster home care, it is more often than not a permanent status for the child.

About 68% of the children have been in foster home care between 4 and 8 years. The average length of time spent in foster home care is more than 5 years, yet 83% of the children have never been returned to their parents, not even for trial periods.

There are substantial reasons, having very little to do with the specific problems precipitating the placement, which caused most biological families to be at risk with respect to the necessity of surrending their child. The data gathered from biological parents and foster parents show that the former are much lower on the socio-economic scale and significantly more disadvantaged than the foster parents. Over 60% of the biological parents have incomes of less than $5,000 a year and 37% earn less than $3,000. Over 67% are either unemployed or hold unskilled labor jobs and almost 70% have never finished high school. Most foster parents have graduated from high school and the fathers are generally employed in a skilled trade. Compared to the typical foster family which earns between $7,000 and $10,000 per year, 40% of the biological families receive public assistance. Eighty-six percent of the foster families own their own home and they are quite stable— 70% have not moved for at least five years. The conclusion is that though both the biological and foster families are part of the same general socio-economic class, the biological families are at the very bottom of the ladder.

Foster home care is clearly a poor people's program. The sobering fact of the matter is that the State and Federal governments have never adequately provided support for services. The problems of poor housing, poverty, lack of medical care, inadequate education, unemployment, and discrimination are the primary causes of parent–child separations in most cases. Regardless of the quality of preplacement services and supervision, these problems will exist. The fact of the matter, therefore, is that so long as dire human needs are unattended to, no amount of family services will be successful in keeping families together.

2. Special Needs and Disabilities

Children in foster home care do not receive adequate diagnostic and/or treatment services.

These children represent a "population at risk." As such, it is likely that they may be in need of special services at a much higher rate than most children. Twenty-five percent of the disabilities have never been evaluated, and of those which have been evaluated, over 1/4 have not had the recommended treatment program implemented. Although Department policies require it and Title XIX (Medicaid) provides the funds to obtain services, there is no established process to assure that every child will be examined by qualified personnel to determine the existence of medical, dental, psychological, and educational problems. Even when such problems are identified, there is no mechanism to guarantee that the children are adequately treated or, for that matter, treated at all.

3. Parental Responsibility and Adoption

The procedures of the Division of Family and Children's Services have permitted 70% of the parents to maintain parental rights without demonstrating significant interest in their children.

Seventy percent of the parents have not seen their child for 6 months or more. Fifty-seven percent of the parents have not seen a social worker for 6 months or more, and over half of this percentage say they "never" see a social worker. Since the Division has no clear policy which specifically defines when a child is considered to be adoptable, this situation continues to exist.

The Division does not move effectively to free children for adoption.

The Division has no effective procedures for assuring that cases where parents appear to be uninterested in their children are reviewed for possible adoption. Even in 40% of the cases where social workers have determined that adoption is appropriate, the Division has failed to take action. In the cases where 210 petitions a legal process abrogating parental rights have been filed, 1/2 have been in the courts for a year or more with no action.

4. Recruitment, Processing, and Training of Foster Parents

The Division does little to prepare or support foster parents.

According to the Division's own standards, 20% of the foster homes used by them are overcrowded as they contain more than 6 children under the age of 16. At the same time, it was shown that over 100 foster parent applications have not been acted upon in just the two regional offices that provided the information. Less than 1/4 of the foster parents received any training prior to receiving their first foster child and the vast majority of these were employed by private agencies. Three-quarters of the foster parents were either completely unaware or did not realize the extent of the child's problems prior to the placement. Twelve percent of the foster parents never even talked to the social worker before the child was placed. In spite of these conditions, the foster parents are forced into assuming major responsibilities without the necessary authority or training to know how to obtain whatever services are necessary. At the time of this study, the Division did not even provide liability insurance to the foster parents.

5. Administrative

The Division has no effective administrative tools to identify the needs of children in their care or to effectively report the nature of its activities.

Much of the information needed for the completion of this study was unavailable as a matter of standard practice. Data on the number of foster homes being supervised, the number of approved spaces in the homes, and the number of children waiting for foster home placements were only available from two regional offices. In spite of numerous efforts on the part of the Project staff, data from the other offices could not be gathered. Although this situation was reported and discussed with the Division's central office administration, the data were still unobtainable.

Obtaining services for children is one particular area where this lack of accountability is a problem. For instance, a social worker may request that a child be provided with special medical treatments. The authorizations may or may not be provided by a number of supervisors to whom the social worker relates, but there is no one person in the Department who is finally responsibile. The consequences are that no person in authority really knows the need for homemakers, speech therapists, psychological evaluations, and medical appliances.

The issue of records and procedures is another area of significant concern. It was found that many of the records of the children do not contain such information as medical records or school records, and as such are incomplete. There is apparently no standardized procedure to assure that these records are obtained. Once obtained, there is no assurance that it follows the child to his placement. Even in the cases where the information has been secured, it was discovered that many of the children's records are filed in cardboard boxes in a closet for lack of space or personnel to file them appropriately.

SPECIFIC FINDINGS

Pertaining to the foster children:

1. 91% are in the caseload of the Division of Family and Children's Services, i.e., are provided with services in the public sector
2. 67% who are in the care of private agencies are supported by the Department of Public Welfare
3. The average age is 10.5 years
4. 77.3% are white; 14.8% are black; and 1.8% are Spanish-speaking
5. 59.7% are Catholic; 35.1% are Protestant; and .7% are Jewish
6. 53% are placed voluntarily; 30% are referred through district courts; and 8% are placed through probate courts
7. Half their fathers, even when available, are not involved in the placement process

8. 35.6% entered care for reasons having nothing directly to do with them such as divorce of parents, desertion, parent in jail, etc.
9. 23% are placed in care as the result of mental illness of a parent; 13.6% as a result of neglect, abuse, or inadequate home; 9.5% as a result of divorce or desertion of the parent (s)
10. 25% were placed as a result of parent incapacitation
11. The average placement has been more than 5 years; about 68% have been in care 4–8 years
12. 16% have been in care before; 10% have been placed four or more times
13. 83% have never been returned to their parents, not even for a trial period
14. Less than 30% have seen their biological parents within the last 6 months
15. 29.7% are reported to be unadoptable because their parents are interested in them; 11.5% because they are too old; 6.4% because a good foster home adjustment has been made; 4.9% because of severe handicaps; and 3.1% because the child does not want to be adopted
16. Of those cases marked "unadoptable due to parental interest," there are almost as many instances where parents have not seen their children for at least 6 months (or where the social worker does not know when the parent last saw them) as there are parents who see their children twice a month or more
17. 357 who are "unadoptable because they have adjusted well to foster home care," would have likely adjusted equally as well to an adoptive home
18. Although 676 are considered to be "unadoptable because they are too old," 17% of them are less than 12 years old

19. 42% are not free for adoption but could have had the legal process started over a year ago; 24% of the delays are attributed to staff shortages

20. 775 are free for adoption; 1/3 have been free for 5 years or more

21. Almost 75% will have to be freed for adoption through the courts

22. 40% who need to be freed through the courts have not been referred to the Legal Department

23. 1/2 of the petitions freeing the children for adoption were filed in court more than 1 year prior to the study but nothing has been done about them

24. Less than 19% of the children who are free for adoption have been referred to the Massachusetts or national adoption resource exchanges

25. About 30% have either not been seen by a social worker for at least 6 months or it is not known when he was last seen

26. About 70% have either been in a social worker's caseload less than 1 year or have been uncovered

27. 1,690 children, over 1/3 of the Department's caseload, are uncovered; that is, have no social worker assigned to them

28. Those who do not have social workers are more likely to remain in care longer than those who do

29. Those who have social workers are more likely to be adopted than those who do not

30. 1/3 have been moved from one foster home because of a behavior problem and were moved for that same reason from the previous foster home

31. 16% of the children who are over 2 years old are in overcrowded foster homes

32. 22% are experiencing school problems

33. 40% are disabled

34. About 1/3 of the disabled present behavior/emotional problems; 18.5% exhibit indications

of mental retardation; 12.7% have some general medical problem

35. Almost 1/4 of the disabled have never been evaluated

36. Of the disabled who have been evaluated, more than 1/4 have not had the recommended treatment program implemented

Pertaining to the biological parents:

1. 37.6% could not be located
2. 1/2 are divorced or separated
3. Over 60% have incomes of less than $5,000 per year; 37% earn less than $3,000 per year
4. 25% reported that financial problems made placement necessary
5. Over 67% are either unemployed or hold unskilled labor jobs
6. Almost 70% have never finished high school
7. 40% receive public assistance
8. The average family has five children and the vast majority of parents are not living together
9. They reported, on an average, more than three children in foster home care
10. 20% have surrendered one or more children for adoption
11. In 63.1% of the time, any one biological family placed more than one child in a foster home; the siblings were placed in the same foster home 45% of the time
12. The parent's inability to control their child's behavior accounted for 12% of the placements
13. Only 1/2 of the children who had ever been returned to them received follow-up care; as a result, almost all the children returned to a foster home

14. Almost 30% felt that placing their child in a foster home was unnecessary

15. 23.3% stated that placement could have been avoided if they had been able to receive quicker or more family counseling

16. Parents reported that having a homemaker would have prevented placement in 17% of the cases

17. 28.8% stated that accessibility to day care would have prevented the placement

18. Over 93% reported that there was virtually no consideration of ways to keep their children home

19. 20% felt that they were not given a realistic picture of foster home care before the placement

20. 43% reported that social workers did not talk to them at all about what foster home care would be like for the child

21. 82% had not met the foster parents prior to the placement of their child

22. 60% felt excluded from participating in the foster home care placement process with their child

23. About 12% are considering surrendering their child for adoption but have not yet done so

24. 75% stated that they would never consider foster care for their children again, even if faced with a situation which made it appear necessary

25. About 60% felt that they do not see their child enough

26. 37.5% of those who feel as though they do not see their child enough state that the social worker prohibits them from doing so; 20% are discouraged by the foster parents; and 20% cannot see their child often enough because the foster home is too far away

27. 31% report they never see a social worker at all; 57% have not seen one for at least 6 months

28. Almost 60% were in contact with the foster care agency for 2 weeks or less before the placement actually occurred; over 3/4 were in contact with the agency 3 months or less
29. 82% saw a social worker six times or less before their child left home
30. 17% stated that they have no intention of taking their child back home
31. 3/4 stated that their social workers are either doubtful about the return of their child or are clearly against it
32. By the time the biological parents were interviewed, 21 children had been returned home; positive changes were reported in 11 cases

Pertaining to the foster parents:

1. 20% of the foster homes are overcrowded
2. The average mother is about 46 years old; the father is less than a year older
3. 81% report intact marriages
4. 82% are white; 15% are black
5. Almost all black foster children are placed with black foster parents
6. The typical family earns between $7,000 and $10,000 per year
7. Most have graduated from high school and the fathers are generally employed in a skilled trade
8. 86% own their home
9. Over 70% have not moved for five years or more
10. 12% of the foster children included in the sample were originally placed with them for a specified period of time, projected to be an average of 9 weeks; the average length of placement has actually been more than 3 1/2 years
11. 36% had met the foster child prior to the placement

12. In 12% of the cases, the social worker did not talk to them about the child prior to the placement
13. 3/4 were either completely unaware or did not realize the extent of the foster child's disability at the time of the placement
14. They reported that 13% of the disabled children had still not been evaluated at the time of the interviews
15. Less than a quarter reported that they had received any foster care training prior to accepting their first foster child
16. More than 93% report that they must regularly use their own financial resources to cover expenses for their foster child

After completing a study such as this, it is perhaps too easy to point to the multitude of problems which have been uncovered and decry the lack of responsibility which may have allowed them to occur. It must be kept in mind, however, that this study, which has been conducted on an entire population of children in foster home care in a state, is the first of its kind. The Massachusetts Department of Public Welfare should be commended for allowing these problems to be aired rather than continuing to keep them hidden as has been done in so many other states.

As with most studies which come out of field practice, it is likely that many of the problems identified above will not be surprising. Though the frequency of problems has not been known, most child welfare specialists have at least been aware of their existence. It is that fact which is most discouraging, for there does not appear to be any activity in the Division of Family and Children's Services to change the practices which allow the problems to continue unchecked.

In fairness to the Department's personnel, it should be remembered that over the last few years they have had to function significantly understaffed. The Department of Public Welfare is constantly under attack from all sides. Their mandate is such that they must take on responsibility for all families and children that other departments and agencies neglect. In spite of these facts, however, many of the problems uncovered in this study could have been dealt with administratively before this.

RECOMMENDATIONS

The recommendations contained herein can be implemented either by the Department itself or through purchase-of-service contracts. Though many believe that the latter is more efficient, that belief must be tempered by fact. In the first place, about half the referrals for foster home care come from social agencies. They were obviously unable to prevent the necessity of the placement. Another fact is that there are no real assurances that if thousands of children were to be placed in private agency care, those agencies would be able to do any better than the Division has done. The fact that 27 licensed child care agencies seem to provide better care for 507 children than the Division of Family and Children's Services does for 5,426 children, does not mean that the private agencies could maintain better control when operating under the same pressures. Finally, it is clear that most agencies have consistently deferred to the Division when foster care is necessary, especially for a child who is older or with special needs.

Private agencies, on the other hand, have more control over their personnel and resources. They have more flexibility in employing staff and establishing subcontractual and/or cooperative agreements with other organizations to provide necessary services. Finally, they are to some extent, albeit slight, more community-based. For example, at the time of this study the Department's decentralization took the town of Norwell from the Brockton regional office, about 15 miles away, and moved it to New Bedford, about 60 miles away.

It is considered that the following recommendations can be quickly implemented. In most cases, they require some reorganization of services and coordination of units. Some may require legislative action, particularly where additional funding is necessary.

1.   Special (Working) Task Force

There is an urgent need to individually review those children who have been virtually imprisoned in foster home care and deprived of services. Once these problems are identified, there must be an assurance that they will be rectified. This must be accomplished immediately.

> It is recommended that a special task force, staffed by social workers and attorneys, review each child's case individually and identify those services necessary to free them from permanent foster care. Once services are named, they should be reported to the commissioner. Responsibility for the case should then return to the social worker. Assurance that the necessary services have been provided should be reported to the commissioner within a specified time.

The cases appearing to be in particular need of review are:

a.   2,945 children, not free for adoption, who have not seen their parents or guardian for 6 months or more,

b.   375 children who are not available for adoption because they have "adjusted well to foster home care,"

c.   127 children who have not been adopted by their foster parents because they do not have enough income to support another child,

d. 676 children considered to be "too old" to be adopted,

e. 288 children considered to be "too handicapped" to be adopted,

f. 667 children who should have had the adoption process started one year ago or more,

g. 592 children free for adoption but not referred to Massachusetts Adoption Resource Exchange or Adoption Resource Exchange of North America,

h. 347 children for whom 210 petitions were filed one year ago or more but no action has been taken,

i. children with 903 disabilities which have not been evaluated,

j. children with 496 treatment programs recommended but never implemented.

This procedure represents a short term solution. It will, however, at least provide some degree of assurance that these children do not continue to be severely neglected by the institution mandated to provide their care.

2. Prevention of Foster Home Care Placements

Preventing the placement of children presumes that the social workers have access to adequate resources. Large numbers of parents felt that alternatives such as homemakers, day care, and family counseling, would have prevented the necessity of surrendering their children.

At present, the Department of Public Welfare purchases a great deal of day care and homemaker services in communities around the state. Under the provisions of Title IV–A, Donated Funds Program, the Department purchases family counseling services. No part of these services, however, is directly affiliated with the Division of Family and Children's Services once a contract is negotiated. The consequence is that the Division's personnel do not have ready access to them in order to attempt prevention of the child's placement.

> It is recommended that the personnel of the Division of Family and Children's Services have homemakers, day care, intensive family counseling services, and others available to them in order to prevent the surrender of a child to foster home care.

In addition, the Division's administration will need to institute mechanisms to insure that alternatives to placement are, in fact, investigated. That aspect will be addressed in a following section on the child care information system.

At present one of the problems in the Division is that none of the administrators has any way of knowing what types of services are needed and how often. In addition, they do not know how often such services are unobtainable as a result of lack of funds, waiting lists, unwillingness of service organizations to accept "welfare cases," etc.

> In order to assure that these services are available on a continuing basis, it is recommended that a central office administrator be designated as the individual who tracks such needs. For instance, if a social worker in a district office is unable to obtain a homemaker, that request would ultimately end up with the designated administrator. This way, even if the particular service could not be obtained, the Division's administration would know which needs are not being met and the size of the problem. With the appropriate information, they could move to fill those gaps in service.

3. Intake and Biological Parent Responsibility

The problems associated with the care of foster children are largely due to the inadequate intake policies and procedures utilized by the Division of Family and Children's Services. These problems consist of: 1.) biological parent responsibility; 2.) medical, dental, psychological, and educational screening; 3.) legal status determination; and 4.) administrative control. Each of these elements will be considered under separate recommendations.

From the perspective of the responsibility of biological parents, it is clear that the present system of surrendering a child to foster home care is inadequate. The system encourages parents to abandon their children without the stigma of having legally done so. One consequence is that less than 30% of the children have seen a parent within 6 months and yet only 775 children are free for adoption.

It is recommended that once it has been established that a child cannot remain in his own home, the process of surrender be changed to include a written agreement, signed by the parent(s), stating their commitment to continuing responsibility for the child. The agreement should specify:

a. How often the parent agrees to see the child and how long the visits will be
b. How much the parent will pay toward the support of the child while in a foster home
c. The parent's responsibility for taking the child to physician, dentist, and other appointments
d. The parent's responsibility for continuing contact with the child's school
e. The parent's responsibility with regard to participating in a treatment program for his or her own problems
f. Other responsibilities to be negotiated

It is recommended that the Department's policies be changed so that a child can only be taken into foster home care, under voluntary status, for a period of 6 months without renewal of the agreement.

The agreement could be updated and changed periodically, as appropriate. Its main purpose would be to negotiate continuing parent responsibility. Given the time limitation of the placement, the agreement would provide the opportunity for the Department to review the degree to which the parent has met or not met the provisions of the agreement. If a parent has not met them, this will be a clear indication that the child has been abandoned. In those cases, the Department can then move expeditiously for the abrogation of parental rights. The social worker will not have to struggle with the question of whether or not the parent maintains interest in the child. The agreement should be so precise that the parents would be aware of the Department's action in the event they fail to maintain the responsibilities agreed upon previously. In addition, such a written agreement would provide the Department's legal staff with substantial evidence when a petition is brought forward in court.

Related to the above issues, a serious problem exists when the removal of a child from a family creates comfort instead of discomfort for the family. The parent may be reluctant to have the child returned home. Continuing and active parental responsibility is the only way to assure that a parent does not eventually reach a point where it is aversive to reunite the family.

> It is recommended that the Department involve biological fathers in the foster home care placement process in every case where he can be contacted.

His signature should appear on the necessary forms or there should be an explanation on the form as to why it does not appear. The policies of the Department, in turn, will need to operationally define the circumstances which will allow placement to occur without his participation.

Finally, these procedures are futile if there is no way of knowing the degree to which a parent is meeting the designated responsibilities. This issue will be addressed in the section on the child care information system.

4. Medical, Dental, Psychological, and Educational Screening

One of the most serious problems identified in this study is the frequency with which disabled children are placed in foster home care and the haphazard manner in which their disabilities are treated. This situation is especially unconscionable because the Department already has the capacity of paying for such screening services through Title XIX (Medicaid) and, in fact, is mandated to do so under United States Department of Health, Education, and Welfare regulations.

> It is recommended that the Division of Family and Children's Services immediately identify comprehensive medical centers around the Commonwealth which show interest in contracting to provide screening services for children about to enter, or recently entering, foster home care. In cooperation with the Division of Medical Assistance, seven facilities, one in each region, should be put under contract to provide comprehensive screening for each child.

The screening should consist of those necessary elements called for in the United States Department of Health, Education, and Welfare regulations and a complete written report on every child should be assured. The report should list the results of the screening and, most important, those additional services necessary to ameliorate any handicapping conditions the child has.

This screening should be prerequisite to placement and, in no case, should it be accomplished later than 2 weeks after a child has been in a foster home. The services identified as necessary for the child would be tracked by the child care information system to be discussed in a later recommendation.

5. Legal Status Determination

Large numbers of children placed in foster home care under voluntary status have, in fact, been abandoned by their parents. Once the child is in care, the parent never sees him. Assuming that the Division implements the recommendations regarding biological parent responsibility, the legal staff will be called upon more frequently to institute proceedings to abrogate the rights of the parents. In this way, at the point of intake, and periodically thereafter, the relationship of the parents to the child can be determined. The child's legal status should be consistent with that relationship.

These procedures create a heavier load for the Department's legal staff. Almost 40% of the 210 petitions which need to be filed for children identified as having been abandoned by their parents, have not yet been filed. In addition, 1/2 of the petitions freeing children for adoption were filed more than 1 year ago but nothing has been done with them. These are but two of the many situations which illustrate that the legal staff of the Department, specifically those assigned to the Division of Family and Children's Services, is woefully undermanned.

There are only two lawyers, one full-time and one half-time, assigned to the D.F. and C.S. Furthermore, they do not have enough secretarial assistance. In the course of this study, it was discovered that submission of final adoption petitions to the probate courts is approximately 8 months behind. This is, allegedly, because there is only one secretary to accomplish this work and she cannot keep up with the demands.

> It is recommended that additional legal staff be employed immediately, with additional secretarial assistance, and be assigned to the Division of Family and Children's Services.

Some of these attorneys should, in turn, be assigned to the special task force mandated to clear the problems identified previously.

6. Foster Parent Responsibility

The current system of foster home care is based upon the assumption that foster parents will provide simple custodial care of children and all decisions pertaining to services for the child will be made by the social worker. This is true in spite of the fact that the foster parents are forced into assuming major responsibility without the necessary authority. In turn, this creates a great difference between the ways that foster parents obtain services for their biological child and their foster child.

> It is recommended that foster parents be authorized to obtain necessary diagnostic and treatment services for their foster child.

This necessitates that the Division establish a clear set of guidelines and procedures for foster parents for making decisions regarding the needs of the foster child.

Foster parents need to be sensitive to the special needs of children. Once the foster parent identifies a problem, she must know how to obtain the necessary services while remaining consistent with Department policy.

> It is recommended that every foster parent complete a training program geared to giving them the skills necessary for identifying and meeting the needs of their foster children.

A second issue with respect to foster parent responsibility is the lack of definitive differentiation between regular and specialized foster home care. There does not appear to be any mechanism to determine whether a child is in need of surrogate family care in a secure, nurturing environment, or a family which has a high tolerance level and the ability to cope with special physical, emotional, or other handicaps. Though some foster parents are paid substantially higher rates than others and are designated as "special" or "professional" foster parents, there is no available, let alone required, special training. These designations seem to be completely unrelated either to what the foster parents do or with whom they do it.

> It is recommended that the Department establish the criteria to define a "special needs child." This child should be maintained in a specialized foster home setting only so long as the special need exists.

Once the child in the specialized foster home is no longer considered to have special problems, he should be moved to a regular foster home or some other less restrictive setting.

> It is recommended that specialized foster homes be those which employ professional foster parents, defined as one who assumes the role of foster parent on a full-time basis. Compensation must be commensurate with time and effort. In addition, each professional foster parent must successfully complete a prescribed training program which would need to be designed and staffed by the Department or contracted out to a private organization.

The professional foster parents should also be required to participate in on-going Department programs and be required to complete periodic reports on their activities and changes in the children under their care.

The foster parents are increasingly being requested to care for older children who, in many cases, present severe behavioral problems. As a result, they are considerably more vulnerable to damages these children may do in their homes, such as fire or theft. Natural parents and even foster children are filing law suits to a much greater degree than they have in the past.

At the same time, many insurance companies consider foster parents to be in the "business" of child care and designate the foster families as "high risk." Consequently, many foster parents do not have liability coverage and are not aware of it. The Commonwealth does not provide insurance coverage to the foster parent.

> It is recommended that foster parents be provided with adequate liability insurance to protect them for property damage and/or personal injury caused by a foster child and/or from legal damages resulting from lawsuits pertaining to the care of the child.

Insurance for such situations is being purchased by some private agencies and the cost is generally between $7 and $10 per year. It is written in addition to the foster parent's homeowner's insurance and becomes primary when there is no homeowner's policy in existence. The policy is specifically for foster children and does not cover the biological children in the family.

7. Foster Parent Monitoring

A minimal amount of work with the biological family of the child is performed. This is partly due to the amount of time which social workers must spend on administrative details relating to the foster parent, foster home, and foster child.

> It is recommended that foster parent monitoring units be established in each regional office of the Department. The staff of these units should carry responsibility for maintaining contact with the foster parent, directly as well as through the use of reporting forms.

They would deal with issues related to policy and service provision. By doing so, a relatively small number of social work personnel can give family workers more time to spend on the resolution of problems which led to the foster home placement.

8. Special Needs Unit

One of the most serious problems discovered in this study was that pertaining to the care of the disabled child. Approximately 40% of the children in foster home care have some disability. 15% have multiple handicaps. Almost 1/4 of the children have never had these handicaps evaluated. Of those children who have been evaluated and had a treatment program recommended for them, over 1/4 have not had the treatment programs implemented.

For approximately 2 years before this study, the Department had a contractual agreement with at least one prepaid health maintenance organization. In spite of this fact, however, large numbers of children were not using that facility and were not receiving the medical services they require.

> It is recommended that a special needs unit be established to take on the function of insuring that children needing special services receive them.

In addition to its monitoring function, the unit would act as liaison with vendors of service. The medical, dental, psychological, and educational screening program should be the responsibility of this unit.

Following publication of the original foster home care study report in 1973, Governor Francis Sargent appointed a committee to oversee implementation of the recommendations. That committee broke down into various task forces, one of which focused on the provision of special services to children with special needs.[1]

It is important to note that the data collected in these studies demonstrated conclusively that even very severely disabled children are currently being cared for in foster homes. A foster home provides a substitute family for a child whose needs, for whatever reason, cannot be met by his natural parents. The foster family, therefore, assumes the responsibility for the care of that foster child. Some of the child's needs will be medical. In a family that functions adequately, the foster parents will meet these needs and in turn select a pediatrician or family physician to manage the medical care of the child.

A child in foster home care has the same right to good medical care as any other child and deserves the same access to medical services. Thus the following recommendations for the treatment and evaluation of foster children in care were made. They are based upon the firm assumption that each child in foster care needs at least two surrogates, someone *in loco parentis* and someone *in loco medico.* Though these recommendations are positive for all children in foster home care, they are viewed as absolutely necessary for the developmentally disabled child.

From the overall perspective, it would appear as though the current policies of the Massachusetts Department of Public Welfare regarding the medical care of foster children were quite adequate, but they do not appear to be implemented by the Department's personnel.

It is recommended that the current policy for medical care of children in foster care be aggressively implemented with the recommended revisions stated in this report.

The revisions recommended are as follows:

1. The initial comprehensive medical examination should be consistent with the Early Periodic Screening Diagnosis and Treatment (EPSDT) Guidelines established by

the Department of Public Welfare and shall include at least the following:

    a. Health history

    b. Immunization record

    c. Present physical condition including growth and development, visual and auditory acuity, nutritional status, dental status, and evidence of communicable disease.

    d. Negative tubercular skin test or chest x-ray

    e. Referral for dental examination and treatment plan

    f. Recommendations regarding permitted or restricted activities

    g. Recommendations regarding care, examinations, treatment, or immunizations

2. Every child in foster care should have a medical examination according to EPSDT Guidelines at least at the following intervals:

Age of Child	Examination Frequency
Birth to 6 months	Every 8 weeks
6 months to 1 year	Every 3 months
1 year to 2 years	Every 6 months
3 years and over	Annually

Every child in foster care after the age of 3 should have a dental examination every 6 months.

Another area of great concern was the intake process for children. The following provision should be included in the intake process for foster care in order to accurately record each child's medical history and to facilitate medical evaluation and future treatment of any health problems.

It is recommended that no child should be accepted into foster care without a current medical history.

Wherever relevant, reports from previous health professionals should be part of the child's medical history. Exceptions should be made only for emergencies and unusual cases.

> It is recommended that each child in foster care should have an initial comprehensive medical examination within 3 days prior to foster home placement or no later than 10 days following foster home placement.

The intake social worker should be responsible for arranging this medical examination and should assist in transporting the child to the medical provider if necessary.

> It is recommended that prior to the Department's acceptance of a child for foster care in both voluntary and court committed cases, the parents should be required to delegate to the Department, by means of a written agreement, the responsibility for the child's medical care as necessary.

For the purposes of treatment of foster children, major medical care can be defined as surgery and/or hospital care. Routine medical care shall be concerned with health maintenance and minor intercurrent illnesses which can be treated in a physician's office. The biological parents should be notified wherever possible prior to the provision of any medical care which is not routine or emergency. By means of its overall written agreement with the foster parent, the Department should delegate the power to authorize necessary medical care. In order that the foster parent be aware of this subdelegation, this must be explicitly stated in the written agreement between the Department of Public Welfare and the parent.

To implement the recommendation that the initial comprehensive medical examination be accomplished prior to foster care placement, the Department of Public Welfare must adopt the policy of obtaining the voluntary placement agreement first. This will facilitate payment for such an examination. In the event that foster placement does not result, the legal parent must understand that the voluntary agreement can be terminated.

> It is recommended that no child should be placed in foster care for reasons of financial burden or health needs. But placement for health reasons and finances when it relates to the provision of health care should be available when medically recommended.
>
> It is recommended that *one* health care provider be identified to assume the responsibility for health care for each child in foster care.

One of the great problems in the care of children with special needs is that health records do not seem to exist and certainly do not travel with the child as he or she changes settings. In addition to health records which the physician keeps for his own files, each child should have a simple, comprehensive health report completed in triplicate at each visit to a health provider. This report should be signed and dated by the attending physician or other health professional. The foster parent should retain one copy and forward the other two copies to the Department. The Department would file one in the foster child's case record and send the other copy to the regional monitoring unit. The copies maintained by the foster parent should accompany the child in the event he moves to another foster home. These health records should be kept with the foster parent's authorization for emergency medical care. The foster parent should also maintain a child's basic baby records in order that the foster child have some record of his own growth and development. This material should also accompany the foster child wherever he goes.

> It is recommended that the Department of Public Welfare maintain the health records for each child in foster care.

Each foster child's health file should include at least the following:

a. The signed authorization by the parent for the provision of medical care
b. The complete report of the initial comprehensive medical examination with referrals and recommendations
c. The copies of the periodic health report, dated and signed by the physician, which were received from the foster parent
d. Any other reports of treatment
e. Records of dental care including medication
f. Records of mental health treatment

> It is recommended that the Department of Public Welfare appoint a health care coordinator for all children in foster care in the Department's Division of Social Services at the central office.

This coordinator should be responsible for the management and monitoring of health care of the children in foster care. The coordinator should have a direct link with the Division of Medical Assistance at central office.

The coordinator should have a person in each region responsible for the management and monitoring of the health care of the foster child in that region. This regional person should receive all copies of health reports from the foster parent and feed the information appropriately into the monitoring system at central office when it is established.

This monitoring system at central office should track all children in foster care by recording such information as location of foster home, financial data, school attendance, health care treatment, and referrals. When a region provides data to the monitoring system on recommended medical treatment for a foster child, and no follow-up report is recorded within a reasonable amount of time, the coordinator at central office should inform the regional staff person. The regional staff person should, in turn, investigate the individual situation. The monitoring system is the most important element in maintaining an adequate health care system. It will be extremely valuable in evaluating, researching, and planning the provision of medical services and finances needed to provide health care to all children in foster care.

One of the universal difficulties of providing medical services to foster children has been the delay of Medicaid reimbursement for health provider bills. These difficulties have interrupted and often impeded necessary medical care to welfare recipients.

> It is recommended that special emphasis be placed on ways to expedite the medicaid vendor payment system.

This will assure the cooperation of health care providers for children in foster care. Most of the recommendations related to this hinge on the Department of Public Welfare's responsibility to pay for services rendered by its health providers.

9. Social Work Staff

As of the date of original publication of this report, the Division of Family and Children's Services was approximately one-third below its normal complement of personnel. One-third of the children did not have social workers assigned to their cases on November 18, 1971. Since that time, the Department has been through two personnel freezes, one internal and the other mandated by the Massachusetts Executive Office of Administration and Finance. The proportion of uncovered cases is certainly higher today than it was then.

At this time, the social worker is the only safeguard available to provide even minimal assurance that a child's needs are met while in foster home care. There are significant differences in how a child receives necessary services, based upon whether or not the case was covered.

> It is recommended that a social worker be assigned to every family and child in foster home care.

This will obviously necessitate the hiring of additional personnel or the provision of funds for purchase-of-service agreements. The failure to provide the funds to do so would constitute a blatant disregard for the lives of these children. Without such coverage, these youngsters are relegated to failure and other studies have shown that many will end up as the responsibility of other departments, such as Corrections or Mental Health, later in their lives.

Finally, there is serious lack of good judgment on the part of some of the social work staff. Of the children who need to be freed for adoption through the courts, 40% have not been referred. Although 11% of the biological parents or guardians have not seen their child for 6 months or more, their child is still designated as "unadoptable due to parental interest." 17% of the children are designated as "unadoptable because they are too old" but are 12 years old or less.

> It is recommended that the Division institute a training program to assure that the social work personnel are acquainted with the necessary criteria to establish plans for children. In addition, an adequate program of supervision and accountability should be instituted.

10. Administration

The Division of Family and Children's Services functions with unspecific policies that are subject to constant interpretation in too many cases. For example, a current policy may state that a child should be considered for adoption release when there is no longer any expression of parental interest. In contrast, an explicit, operational policy might be as follows: "Any child in the care of the Massachusetts Department of Public Welfare, not freed for adoption, whose parent(s) or legal guardian have not visited the child for a period of 12 consecutive months, will be referred to the Legal Department for the filing of a 210 petition. Exception to this policy shall be made only in the event of mitigating circumstances and authorized by the Director of Family and Children's Services on Department Form ABC. This authorization must be renewed every 3 months. Children not visited by a parent or guardian for a period of 2 years must be referred to the Legal Department unless exception is made by the Commissioner."

An explicit, operational policy, such as above, demands that certain actions be carried out and places the responsibility for such actions directly with particular persons. Such policies must relate to a wide variety of tasks which should be performed by foster parents, social workers, supervisors, "middle management," and administrators.

> It is recommended that the Department review its policies related to the provision of service to children and families and rewrite them in operational form where necessary. In addition, the Department policies should reflect clear lines of responsibility with mechanisms for accountability.

Generally it was found that there are no administrative check-offs to assure that the records of a child contain all the necessary information. Records are often missing school reports, medical information, etc. This information, even when available, is not passed on to the foster parent. The result is that foster parents are faced with the responsibility of caring for a child about whom they know very little.

It is recommended that an administrative check-off system be established to assure that appropriate information on every child in care is obtained. This information should, in turn, be summarized and forwarded to the foster parent.

SPECIAL RECOMMENDATION

Child Care Information, Service, and Cost Accounting System

No amount of reliable information has value unless there are competent administrators to make use of it. It is equally true that the most competent administrators cannot function effectively if they are not aware of the trends and problems in their organization. This is especially true when the administration of an organization does not have a mechanism through which its personnel is accountable for its time and activity.

To assure that the problems identified in this report will not recur once they have been dealt with, the major recommendation of this report is to implement a child care information, service, and cost accounting system. Though such a recommendation is somewhat undramatic, the lack of such a system, even manually operated, is probably the greatest single factor which has allowed the problems to exist.

A monitoring or tracking system, such as is being proposed here, must serve as a tool to expedite decision making and accountability. It should monitor program development, maintain program control, guide staff development, assist in staff deployment, and provide a base for research and evaluation. The primary objective is systematic data collection which will, in turn, enable the Department administrators to effectively improve their decision-making processes and efficiently allocate their resources such as funds and personnel. Thus, with the management greatly improved, the delivery of child welfare services would be considerably more effective.

It takes a combination of concerned and conscientious personnel and a reliable information system to provide the necessary protection for the children in care. It is obviously impossible for even the most conscientious staff member to intervene in unknown problems. Conversely, even when the problems are identified, the personnel must be prepared to deal with them until they are resolved. At the present time, the Division is laboring under the pressure of a double handicap. It has neither the information nor the personnel.

The purpose of a child care information, service, and cost accounting system should be fivefold:

1. To monitor and analyze current Division activity in order to allow effective case tracking. Such data as the following should be collected and reported:
    a. Source of referral
    b. Geographical location of child and family
    c. Family characteristics
    d. Child characteristics
    e. District office assignment
    f. Special problems
    g. Other agency involvement
    h. Time lapsed since referral
    i. Number of times in foster care
    j. Legal status
    k. Parent involvement

2. To project the future direction of the Division and assist in the decision-making processes which will most effectively bring that movement about. For instance, this year, are more or less children being referred by juvenile courts than last year? Does the child placed in a foster

home through a purchase-of-service contract with a private agency stay in foster care for a shorter period of time than his counterpart in a Division foster home? Do children get more medical services when they are provided with such services through a prepaid facility?

3. To collect data regarding service delivery and outcome, such as the following:

    a. Frequency of child–social worker contact

    b. Frequency of child–parent contact

    c. Frequency of parent–social worker contact

    d. Frequency of social worker–foster parent contact

    e. Social worker's activity on behalf of the child and family, i.e., contact with schools, courts, medical personnel

    f. Degree of achievement of specified case goals, e.g., reunification of family within 3 months of entering care; releasing the child for adoption through a 210 petition within 2 months, etc.

    g. Degree of parent satisfaction 3 months after discharge from foster care

4. To utilize cost benefit analysis as an on-going guide toward effective services per dollar. Does it cost more or less for the Department to purchase services from private agencies than if it provided the same services itself? Are the costs for providing the same services different in one region than in another? Has decentralization resulted in the provision of more and better services for the same or less cost?

5. To maintain an on-going data collection system, with assurance of easy retrieval, which can be utilized for research and statistical reports of Division activity. Such a system would, for instance, allow rather simple replication of this study.

The reports generated by this system would then be provided regularly, e.g., monthly, to the responsible persons. In turn, the information would allow them to deploy staff and resources to the problem areas. These reports would contain case-by-case information, as well as aggregate data, to insure that an individual child, who does not conveniently fit a category, would not be lost. An individual child's special need could be identified.

It is almost impossible for the Division to prevent the problems identified in this report from recurring until it has such a system. It is simply a herculean task to assure high quality, comprehensive services to thousands of families and children through the use of manual procedures.

NOTES

1. In addition to the author, the active members of the Task Force on Evaluation and Treatment of Foster Children were: Mel Scovill, Assistant Commissioner for Medical Assistance, Department of Public Welfare; Ann Himmelburger, Massachusetts Foster Parents Association; William Dowling, Supervisor, Department of Public Welfare; Margaret Monnie, Child Welfare Specialist, Department of Public Welfare; Mary Gabrilla, Social Worker, Department of Public Welfare; Barbara Kohlsaat, Lecturer on Social Work, Harvard University School of Public Health; Barbara Cannell, Social Worker, Department of Public Welfare; Phillip Porter, M.D., Cambridge City Hospital.

   Special acknowledgment should go to Cynthia Harvell, the staff member assigned to the Task Force. Along with Ms. Kohlsaat, Ms. Harvell's contributions to the product of the Task Force were invaluable. The recommendations contained herein are the result of considerable effort of the persons mentioned above.

Chapter 8

AFTERWORD

This is certainly not the first study of foster home care to conclude that the system is ineffective. It is not even the first study to conclude that the system does damage to the children. Why then, with all the initial political and professional support for the study, did it fail to affect the manner in which foster home care services are provided to children and their families?

In attempting to answer that question, one is tempted to look at the political process, Federal regulations, fiscal constraints, and other elements. Yet, in reality, it is likely that the explanation for the unresponsiveness of the political and social welfare leadership is based on the simple phenomenon of "issue life," i.e., the period of time which an issue is in the public's eye and susceptible to change.

Concurrent with release of the first study, the Massachusetts Governor's Commission on Adoption and Foster Care issued its official report. That document was based upon the data gathered in the research activities. Subsequent press conferences, radio and television appearances, newspaper stories, and other modes of making the public aware of the status of children in foster care managed to focus interest on the matter for a short while. Once the coverage had run its course, however, the situation returned to a state almost identical to pre-Commission report days. It is a statement of the lack of coordination of the political and social welfare sectors that this problem continued to exist even while they had the opportunity to maximize their collaborative efforts.

There are a plethora of factors to be considered when attempting to establish the realities attendant to changing any system as large and complex as the one in question. At the same time, however, some of the most important realities are more often than not neglected. Some of these are: 1) government policies often change very slowly, 2) children don't stay children forever, 3) adults remain as adults for a long time, 4) adults have a tendency to multiply, and 5) adults tend to parent as they were parented.

Why are these almost too simple notions necessary to repeat? For one thing, they are so simple as to be almost invisible to even the most sophisticated observer. It is important to recognize that contending with the child welfare system is simply not a children's problem. What people fail to consider, almost as if they sometimes didn't know it, is that children grow up. At the same time, the real hooker in this cycle of events is that government resources have a great tendency to remain stagnant. The changes that occur are often minimal, and regrettably, frequently window dressing in order to maintain a facade which is politically expedient. Nonetheless, many of the social problems with which the child welfare system is expected to deal are generational. That is, the children are behaving in a manner which is consistent with the behavior of their parents and other important people in their environment. The result is that we have a much larger group of people suffering the consequences of social neglect while those in positions of political leadership attempt to contain the social programs which they maintain are of great cost to the taxpayer. The ultimate consequence is that we will find ourselves in an increasingly impossible position. We will be attempting to meet the needs of more and more people while failing to increase the resources necessary to deal with those problems or attempting to change the basic format of the services.

This fact is especially clear throughout this report as the data relate to the biological parents of the children in care. The majority of foster parents are highly motivated and well qualified to provide food, shelter and surrogate parenting to the children in their homes. It was shown, for instance, that the average foster parents are in their mid-forties and have already had the experience of raising their own families. Yet, a social worker is assigned to the child to provide "professional" services and, all too often, the social workers are in their twenties, with no parenting experience and presenting as their sole qualification a bachelor's degree in liberal arts. There is also a worker assigned to the family of the child but there is not a shred of evidence to suggest that any realistic attention is paid to the salient fact that the child was removed from home because of the unwillingness or inability of his or her family to provide appropriate parenting. The child obviously will be unable to return to his or her natural home until the conditions which led to the removal are rectified, but these aspects of social services are so minimal as to be nonexistant. The result . . . once a child enters foster care, he or she can expect to be away from home for about five years, and in most cases, until they are well into their adolescence.

The publication of this volume has been delayed for about two years in order to follow the impact of the two research reports on which it is based, *Foster Home Care in Massachusetts: A Study of Foster Children, Their Biological and Foster Parents* and *The Developmentally Disabled Child in Foster*

Home Care. The first report was originally released in March, 1973, and the second in March, 1974.

Compared to 1971, a study of the Massachusetts foster care system in 1976 would reveal that there are no essential differences in the way the Commonwealth deals with children in foster care. Especially with respect to the biological parents of these children, there is every reason to believe that there has been substantial deterioration in the accessibility of and effect of family services.

One of the prime considerations in the quality of any foster care system is the availability of people to deal with the case issues. In the spring of 1973, there were 200 professional child welfare vacancies in the Massachusetts Department of Public Welfare. These vacancies existed because the Governor had placed a freeze on non-essential state jobs because of budget difficulties. When the Commission submitted its report, the Governor announced that he was not only allowing those jobs to be filled but was also authorizing the establishment of a large number of new positions. In Massachusetts, this was after all the "Year of the Child!"

In spite of such statements, the Department of Public Welfare's fifth report to the Governor on the progress of the Commission's recommendations indicated that in August, 1974, 17 months after the release of the Commission's official report, 22 vacancies still remained out of the original 200. This was not to mention the new positions that were supposed to be added!

Even worse, in 1975, 2 years after the Commission's report, the Boston Legal Assistance Project filed suit in the United States District Court against the Massachusetts Department of Public Welfare. The brief, filed by Attorney Gershon Ratner, showed that approximately 20,000 eligible service recipients did not have social workers assigned to their cases. Of that number, 1,530 were children in foster care and 220 were children waiting to be adopted. This was an indication that the Department's uncovered caseload had increased even more since the 1971 data were collected. By this time, according to the brief, there were 142 child welfare vacancies in the Department. Yet, the number of children in foster home care had grown from about 6,000 to almost 8,000 in 1976.

It would be unfair not to acknowledge the gains which the Department staff were able to achieve with their very limited resources and administrative support. A report issued in August, 1974, showed that the following had been accomplished:

1. The Department staff reviewed 890 cases which resulted in the placement of 295 children in adoptive homes, 292 children scheduled to be adopted by their foster parents, and 188 children scheduled for adoption with others.

2. Since the legal staff of the Department had been increased, 428 petitions were brought before the probate courts of the Commonwealth to seek release for adoption. Of that number, 184 children had received decrees but 244 were still waiting for action.

3. By June 30, 1974, the Legal Department had completed 500 adoptions compared to 233 the previous fiscal year.

4. The Department had reduced overcrowding from approximately 20 percent to less than 1 percent. The Massachusetts Office for Children indicates that in 1976, the 7,939 children in foster home care are placed in approximately 3,500 private homes.

5. Foster care payments to foster parents have been raised to $22 per week for a child up to the age of 6, $32 for a child who is 7–12 years old, and $42 per week for a child over the age of 12.

In addition, since that report, about 1/2 the adoptions being consummated in the State involved the foster parents of the child. This is a marked reversal of the previous policy which overtly discouraged such a practice.

Finally, though it has taken about 4 years, the Department is in the process of attempting to establish a system whereby biological parents and foster parents are required to enter into written contractual agreements with the Commonwealth before the child enters a foster home. This contract specifies the rights and responsibilities of the parties and hopefully will reduce the frequency of abandonment of children to the foster care system.

In spite of these gains, the manner in which foster children are cared for in Massachusetts and in most other states is appalling. To provide effective services in any system, good people and good information are necessary. Massachusetts has good people in the Department of Public Welfare but not nearly enough of them. The State certainly does not have anything which even approaches good information. At the same time, the Legislature and Executive Branch of the Commonwealth behave in such a way as to indicate their very low priority given to problems such as identified here.

The original research report emphasized that an effective service accounting, i.e., monitoring system, was a priority. Such a system would allow for periodic review and evaluation of all cases. Administrators and social workers would receive periodically updated information on the status of the children, the placement, the existence of problems, the movement towards specified goals, the contact between child and biological parent, and other important elements. To date, however, though the need for such a system has been oft proclaimed, the Commonwealth's executives and legislators have failed to respond. Obtaining relevant data for individual case decisions, program planning or effective management is as impossible today as in

1971, a fact which must be considered to indicate naivete at best or gross neglect and irresponsibility at worst.

As indicated above, the number of children in foster homes in Massachusetts has increased by about 1/3 since 1971. It seems clear that this growth is inevitable and will probably continue as long as the Commonwealth and the Federal Government continue to cut back support of various human services. In spite of clear evidence that community-based intensive service programs are able to bring about substantial gains, usually at less—certainly at no more—cost than separating a child and family, current Commonwealth and Department administrators continue to cut back such programs.[1] It is almost as if we say to parents, "We know things are bad but just hold on for a while. When they get worse, we'll take your child away from you and then you won't have to worry about him any more."

The fallacy, of course, is that, as indicated above, these children grow up, multiply, and simply present society with much greater problems down the line. If the foster child population continues to grow as it is, then we may well have twice the number of children in foster home care by 1985 as we did in 1971.

The most effective way, if not the only way, to contend with foster care is to prevent it whenever possible. Yet, while the caseload has increased by about 2,000 children, there are essentially the same number of social workers today as there were when there were 2,000 less children in the system. It is virtually impossible for any social worker, no matter how talented and devoted, to provide the necessary services to children, their biological parents and foster parents. Without such services, there is little or no opportunity for the child and parents to be reunited. The child, therefore, is committed to growing up without benefit of biological parents.

At the same time, in order to maintain a "responsible government," i.e., reduce the budget, the Department of

Public Welfare has been substantially reducing its contractual agreements with the private sector. Even contracts known to be effective and economical have been terminated because their elimination will save money. The result is that services are simply not provided at all and the Department's staff do not have the assistance of people from private agencies to deal with the various requests. The result is that even a "band-aid" approach is fast becoming impossible.

Quite recently, the Massachusetts Office for Children (OFC) conducted an unprecedented licensing study of the Department's family foster care program. That study found the Department to be in non-compliance with 186 regulations required by the OFC for licensing approval. It is probably safe to say that if a private agency were found to be in such extreme non-compliance, their license to conduct foster care programs would be suspended, indeed, probably revoked.

Though the citations against the Department are too numerous to array in detail, the following represent just some of the problems uncovered: a) lack of basic record data such as medical records, authorizations and consents, data pertaining to legal actions, etc.; b) lack of evaluations and service plans; c) lack of specification of continuing parental responsibility; d) lack of criteria for selection of foster parents; e) lack of home studies for children placed out-of-state; f) lack of periodic case review; g) uncovered caseloads, i.e., no social worker assigned; h) failure to refer children for adoption, even when parents have not made any effort to contact the child for more than one year; i) lack of termination plans and follow-up; j) failure to provide regular medical examinations; k) failure to provide diagnostic, treatment and consultation services; l) failure to provide services to the child's biological family; and others. This study provides ample evidence to further document the Commonwealth's neglect of these children in spite of knowledge of the facts.

The individual horror stories regarding foster children are legion. They are distributed over the entire area of the State and regardless of the concern of their foster parents, are often nobody's children. Though their placement is usually and ostensibly temporary, there is virtually no attempt to reunite them with their natural families. They are neglected by the very system which was held out to be the child's benefactor.

Foster children have fewer civil rights than almost any other group of human beings. They are separated from their families by a "voluntary" system which is often, in reality, not voluntary for the parents and certainly cannot be construed to be voluntary from the child's point of view. They have no right to counsel, no specific advocate, and no right to judicial review of their status. They often do not have social workers who they actually see and talk to. All too often there has been no parent-child contact for years. The child, therefore, is in limbo. He is simply moving on, waiting to reach majority in order to be discharged from care, and, too often, contribute in turn to the vicious cycle.

There will come a time in this country when we will recognize that dealing with our priorities effectively is not a luxury. We allow ourselves to perpetuate the myth that the primary problems in the foster care system are technical, i.e., we lack the knowledge and skill to improve the services. The fact is that we are faced with a moral, not a technical crisis. The question is not *can* we fulfill our responsibilities to these children and families. The question is *will* we?

Until we are able to answer that question with a resounding yes, the majority of children in foster care will remain destitute, neglected . . . and betrayed.

NOTES

1. Heck, Edward T. and Gruber, Alan R. *Treatment Alternatives Project.* Boston: Massachusetts Department of Public Welfare and Boston Children's Service Association. 1976.

   Jones, Mary Ann; Neuman, Renee and Shyne, Ann W. *A Second Chance for Families: An Evaluation of a Program to Reduce Foster Care.* New York: Child Welfare League of America. 1976.

2. Massachusetts Office for Children. *Part II—Approval Study Report, Department of Public Welfare's Family Foster Care Program.* Mimeo. 1977.

INDEX